# I WILL NOT BE A PAWN

To: SpringHill Production Co.

This is my way of helping communities throughout the country, hope you enjoy the read.

JOSEPH SPICER SR.

Joseph S. Spicer 6/28/19.

ISBN: 1533041946
ISBN 13: 9781533041944

# I WILL NOT BE A PAWN: THE TRUE STORY OF PRISON COVER UP & CORRUPTION

## Chapter 1

# BECOMING A MAN

Chess is a complicated game. The way it works is that every piece moves in a certain way. The pieces can't break their molds or learn or change. The pawn can't learn how to move like a knight, the knight can't learn to move like a rook, and the rook can't learn to move like a queen; that's the difference between people and chess pieces. There's an expression about "being a pawn," but all the pieces are basically pawns, because they can't change. The most important thing I learned while working in the criminal justice system is that it is possible for people to change—for better and worse. People can learn, people can grow, and people can stand up and move in ways more heroic than the shape they might be cast in. This is the story of how I insisted on being a man, on standing up and telling the truth—how I refused to be a pawn.

I'm not an exceptional person; I don't make a fuss over things. I do my job and mind my business. Corrections officers aren't supposed to stand out—you don't go into corrections to get famous or to be celebrated or to stand out as an individual. But sometimes, even though you might not care about standing out, you find yourself standing up and stepping out of your role or what's expected of you. This story is based on actual events that went on during my journey through the Michigan Department of Corrections as a corrections officer. During the last chapters of my twenty-nine-year career, I witnessed a troubling and disappointing pattern of leadership throughout the correctional facility from which I would eventually retire in March of 2015. I witnessed corrupt and unconscionable conduct on the part of guards, supervisors, and wardens. To my knowledge, the supervisory staff at the correctional facility were never disciplined or fired for their behavior and actions; they all were able to walk away as if these situations never existed.

When people ask me if I'm afraid to tell this story, I tell them that if I was afraid of anything, it would've been working in a maximum-security prison with all those lifers. These men had been convicted of violent crimes, and I stood between them and their freedom. Telling my story is easy compared to that. Working in the prison, I was able to have a unique perspective about life, about individuals of all races—whites, blacks, Hispanics—because I worked in a highly intense, highly integrated environment. As an officer, I was also able to step outside that environment, back into the real world of normalcy. I can't tell you how different it was to go from the prison—a place where everyone was out to manipulate you, where you never knew if you could trust someone, where you had to stand between all these men and what they wanted—to go out into the world again, where there was at least some chance that you could trust someone, where you didn't have to be on guard all the time.

Not a lot of people can balance this type of change from one extreme to another. Correctional officers, due to the stress of their jobs in the 1970s and '80s, didn't usually live very long after retiring. Even beyond the '70s and '80s, officers tend to have bad health, which deteriorates due to lack of exercise, overindulgence in alcohol to cope with high stress levels, and unhealthy eating habits over years of working in a high-intensity field. Correctional officers take on immense physical and psychological responsibility. You have to be able to multitask, to dissect situations and behaviors clearly and precisely. This means you need to understand prisoners' mannerisms and moods, but it also means detecting when a prisoner is acting out of his or her normal behavior pattern. Noticing signs like these helps officers survive from day to day in an environment where they are subject to physical danger, emotional manipulation, and bribery, among many other dangers.

Officers and staff would be manipulated due to their close ties with neighborhood friends. They felt like there was an obligation or loyalty to that neighborhood person because they knew him or her on the street. So officers would allow themselves to get comfortable talking to these folks and feel sympathy toward them being incarcerated. Due to that neighborhood connection, they'd be manipulated into bringing things in—drugs, cologne, different items that would range in seriousness. Once the staff had crossed that line, prisoners could manipulate them through blackmail.

"You got me that gum," a prisoner could say. "Why not those cigarettes?"

And then it would escalate.

"You got me those cigarettes; how about some weed? If you can't get me the weed, maybe I'll tell somebody about those cigarettes..."

This threatened the jobs and pensions of officers, and many staff would get stuck in positions where they were doing things they didn't want to do—out of fear.

I am a twenty-nine-year veteran of the Michigan Department of Corrections. I started working for the Department of Corrections at the Marquette Branch Prison in the Upper Peninsula of Michigan in 1986. I worked there for two years. I had just turned twenty-two years old. I had left college, where I had been on a scholarship and had played basketball. As a lifelong athlete, I had seen basketball as a vehicle for pursuing a good quality of life for myself. But by twenty-two the reality of life had started to set in, and I found myself walking into my first prison.

The fact that I was a guard and not a prisoner had a lot to do with my parents and the strong sense of myself I gained from their guidance. I came from an attentive, stable two-parent family. My father was a factory worker and a Korean War veteran. There was a total of twelve children—ten boys and two girls. That might be why I was so eager to go to school and get out of the house. I'm the seventh son, and my brothers all played football. For the most part, they were pretty good at it and went to college on football scholarships. Football was easy for me, and basketball was a challenge. Most of my brothers went to college and came home after one or two years, having fallen in love with girls. They wanted to come home and start families at very young ages. I'm the closest to graduating from college—just thirty credits away. I saved my money and was about to go back and finish in 2001, when the whole world changed. When 9/11 hit, it threw me off of my plan. I had planned to take out a loan from my 401K to pay for college, but the market crashed and shrunk the 401K. I do plan on finishing; that's one of my goals.

My father was a hardworking man, and even though there were twelve of us, we never wanted for anything. All my brothers had the luxury of receiving cars when they graduated from high school. In addition to working at the factory, my father also ran an after-hours liquor and gambling joint in the early 1970s, down in the Brewster projects area. We would see him on the weekends and Mondays. This was the typical hustle of the time for factory workers who had large families. There weren't any real established casinos around during those days in the Detroit area, and most of the factory workers needed a place to go and wind down and enjoy themselves. I can only remember going down to that complex one time, seeing older gentlemen relaxing and drinking and playing cards. This was a common pastime for African American factory workers because they received high wages but had nowhere to spend their extra money and had nothing to do.

By the time I was in middle school, my father had injured himself and couldn't work in the factory anymore. He came home and stayed, permanently. The buck stopped there for me. While my brothers had been able to come and go with total freedom while my father was at work, I couldn't go anywhere without him noticing. Which meant that I couldn't go out and play with the girls at the playground, where they were playing "hide and go get it," kissing and hugging each other at twelve or thirteen years of age.

Of all his children, my father monitored me the most. My brothers started having families at nineteen, twenty, twenty-one, and twenty-two years of age, but I was more goal oriented; I was really focused on what I wanted to do with my whole life. A lot of my insight came from watching my brothers' positive steps and minor slipups, which were mostly due to falling in love and not staying focused on the bigger picture. They would sit me down and talk to me. Even at fourteen or fifteen, I was willing to listen and absorb information, understand right and wrong, and learn how to avoid their mistakes.

This would become important in my growth and maturity and my ability to handle the responsibility of being a correctional officer at such a young age. The most important thing I learned from my brothers was that if there's something you want, you have to work hard to go out and get it. I used to get up early in the morning and work out, which I saw them do my whole life. That practice translated into discipline, and it helped me with self-discipline. When you have self-discipline, you can achieve what you set out to do. My brothers worked hard in sports and were successful, and they went to college. But they became fathers very early and went to work in factories and other places that weren't where they wanted to be instead of graduating from college. They would instruct me about the ways of life, and between their talk's and me watching them, I would understand how to navigate at an early age. I was traveling to different places all on my own, going to basketball camps, and I would pay attention to what folks said and would do. I was raised in a Baptist church, and I knew right from wrong. The climate then was not about drugs, not as messed up as now; the objective was to go to college and get yourself into a nice career. The stories my brothers told me and the work ethics I had developed through sports helped with the discipline I would need and also helped me move forward in my sports career. None of my brothers or sisters were ever incarcerated, so my parents must have done a pretty good job.

I was privileged to be a pretty good basketball player when coming out of high school in Detroit, Michigan, in 1982. I was a point guard, which I didn't like to be called; I liked to be called a player with the ability to do multiple things. I was considered one of the top five players in the city of Detroit and one of the top three point guards in the state of Michigan. I had a very nice set of clippings from *Detroit News* and *Free Press*, and the school I went to would be one of the top high-school teams in the state of Michigan. During the late 1980s, I played against some prominent guys who eventually made it to their utopias—Roy Tarpley (Dallas Mavericks may he rest in peace), Mark Price (Cleveland Caveliers), Kevin Willis (Atlanta Hawks), and a few others.

My basketball travels took me to Louisville, Kentucky, in June 1981, where I met Mark Price at a basketball camp called Cage Scope. In the championship games there, I would take him for granted. It was foolish of me. As I soon learned, you should never underestimate anyone's ability to perform. Jump shots were raining from the sky, and I was saying to myself, "What the hell?" But by then it was too late, and his team had won the championship. I was left to wonder, "How could this skinny-looking guy perform like this?" I said to myself, "My bad, I'll never underestimate anyone again!" I had learned a valuable lesson.

In July of that summer, I attended another high school basketball camp called Five Star, in Pittsburgh, Pennsylvania, at a college on the outskirts of the city. By this time, I had gotten a chance to apply everything I had learned at Cage Scope, and I had practiced at the gym, working on my fundamentals every day. I was not going to take anyone who I would encounter this time lightly. We arrived via a Greyhound bus; as soon as I got off the bus, I was told to put my gym shoes on. There were nine courts connected to each other—full courts. Imagine about 230 campers—basketball players of different nationalities and from areas of the Southeast. Getting singled out or chosen by these camp counselors was the first step of many major division college basketball players, who would go on to become professional basketball players in the NBA. One particular camp counselor selected me. His name was Mark West, and he went to school at Old Dominion College on the East Coast, and he played in the NBA for at least ten years. I remember him playing for the Phoenix Suns in the late '80s. I would not be picked with the first or second draft of camp goers, though, because I didn't dive on the surface of the court. I was shocked to see these guys diving on the surface, and this was a serious matter to those who were at the camp.

My parents paid for me to attend these two camps, but I didn't want to put the burden of paying for more onto them. All the players' families were paying a handsome price to give their children the opportunity to play and develop their skills in these top-notch competitive environments. This was before sponsors entered the arena of high-school sports and before amateur sports became so commercialized. Nowadays, well-known shoe companies are paying for kids to go to sports camps, but when I was growing up, these camps cost us at least $500 each, which didn't include travel to and from the camp.

Eventually, one camp counselor saw something in me and picked me to play point guard on his team. Believe it or not, we would go on to win the championship for this session in July. One of my fondest memories of this camp was when, during the week, the head camp director, whose name was Howard Karfunkle, came over to me and said, "Son, do you know how dangerous you'd be if you got a jump shot?"

Of course, being a cocky seventeen-year-old at the time, I was saying in the back of my mind, "*Please*, I do have a jump shot!"

I didn't say that to him, but I said it to myself.

A little while later, Howard introduced me to a Flint, Michigan, legend, Trent Tucker, who played for the New York Knicks and went to college at the University of Minnesota. Trent Tucker was a masterful shooter. I worked with him on my shooting throughout the week, which helped build my confidence and eventually allowed me to win an award. At the award ceremony, there was a guy named Dick Vitale, who is now a professional college basketball commentator; he coached at the University of Detroit and in the NBA for the Detroit Pistons in the late '70s and for one or two years in the early '80s.

Dick Vitale was the emcee of the award ceremony. Now, remember, I am from Detroit, Michigan—the motor city—and I had gone to Detroit Northwestern, the same high school attended by one of Dick Vitale's most popular players. Dick Vitale coached Terry Tyler, a powerful rebounder and high scorer for the Detroit Pistons for years Dick Vitale coached him both in college and in the pros.

When the time came in the award ceremony to announce the Most Outstanding Player award, Dick Vitale paused and then started saying things I didn't understand. I knew my name was about to be called, but when Vitale saw that I'd also attended Detroit Northwestern, he started saying that I was a "diaper dandy," an "assist machine," and some other jargon that only he could pull off. I received my trophy, but I was left to wonder what "diaper dandy" even meant. Later I found out that this was his way of saying that I was a very good prospect.

Believe it or not, I would go on to sign a few autographs from young kids who were there. Think about it: being seventeen years old and having a few young kids wanting your autograph? The pride and confidence I got from experiences like this would become a problem as I entered my last year of high school, because now I didn't just want a basketball scholarship; I wanted a scholarship from Georgetown University. I was determined not to accept any other offer from any other school. I deeply admired the legendary coach of the Hoyas, John Thompson. I like how they played, and they had a rivalry with North Carolina, where Michael Jordan had played. I would've turned down scholarships from Division Schools, Eastern Michigan, Duquesne, and others, because I was waiting on Georgetown to call. But it would never happen. Remember, I was an impressionable seventeen-year-old kid who was told that he was a "diaper dandy" by Dick Vitale. A few young kids wanted my autograph; it should have been humbling, but it went to my head.

I think I had a chance to get a scholarship from a Division II school called Oakland University in Rochester, Michigan, where the Detroit Pistons were practicing while they played at the Silverdome. I visited the campus and took some classes with the Pistons' cheerleaders.

The coach took me aside and said, "You could spend the night up here, be with these girls."

I thought about this and wondered if the cheerleaders really wanted to have sex with me or if they were just willing to do it to persuade me to accept a position on the team. I said no to spending the night with them and no to attending Oakland University.

Now I know that this was foolish of me. If nothing else, if I had played for them, I would have gotten to play against Isaiah Thomas, an NBA legend, during the summer and spring. What other challenge would I need to push me to be my best?

Never mind the Pistons' cheerleaders.

Anyway, even though I regret the decision not to sign with schools like Oakland, I would still go on to get a scholarship. Ultimately, all the glory of playing professionally didn't matter to me as long as I could fulfill my desire to go to college and pursue a good-quality, comfortable life.

This decision would shape me; I recognized the importance of making the right choice for my long-term goals, especially in regard to those decisions that impacted my life in the long run. We may not be able to control everything that goes on throughout our journey, but we should be able to slow down and put some thought into what we're trying to accomplish. This is very important for young folks today, who are living in the fast-paced digital world, making their big life decisions in this so-called microwave atmosphere. Microwaves are all about being faster, making electric reactions to save time so you can do many other things. But everybody knows that what comes out of the microwave isn't going to be nearly as tasty as what comes out of a real kitchen, made from real ingredients that someone took the time to put together from his or her heart.

Even as a very young person, I worked hard to balance the thoughts I had about sports with the reality of life. Being realistic, I knew that most athletes never got the chance to play in the professional utopias we envisioned for ourselves, where all our dreams come true. But I realized that, like my father, I could control my destiny if I had a good-quality working career. That's what I mean about balancing life and expectations; I managed my expectations and didn't get caught up in the dream of the commercial part of sports. I didn't want fancy cars or mansions or to live in luxury; I just wanted stability so that I could live a good life, and that's why I knew to take the opportunity when I saw it.

I did go on to play a little college basketball, but a different challenge came about while I was home for the winter break, and I decided to take on that challenge. Sorting through my mail, I noticed a letter from the Michigan Department of Corrections about a mass hiring. This was during the drug epidemic in the mid late 1980s. Drugs, especially crack cocaine, were sweeping through this country, definitely throughout Michigan but especially in the Detroit area. The letter went on to say, "You can get full benefits upon retirement; you will be able to retire after twenty-five years of service and collect a check and full health-care benefits." Now, I'm not the smartest guy there is, but I knew that this career in the Department of Corrections would allow me to be able to retire at the young age of fifty-one. I decided to accept this challenge, even though it meant leaving school. I did just that and never looked back. It was a tough decision, but one that I am just as confident about today as I was the day

I made it. I was still waiting on Georgetown University to call—but that wasn't happening.

I started my career at Marquette Branch Prison in the Upper Peninsula of Michigan. Michigan has what's considered two separate lands connected by a long expanding bridge. On one side of the bridge is Lake Huron, and on the other side of the bridge is Lake Michigan. The bottom half of Michigan looks like a mitten, and the top half looks like a rabbit. I would live in the rabbit section for the next two years. At this time, I was one of only five African Americans working in the Michigan prison system as officers. At this time, the so-called drug wars were in full swing, and the number of African Americans in prison had increased dramatically in a very short time. A number of discipline problems, including riots, had arisen because the white prison guards didn't know how to deal with this increase in African American prisoners.

Surprisingly, the prison population itself was about half African American and half white. The black communities are condensed; a lot of them go to prison, and a lot of Caucasians are locked up, which I learned working up north. It was pretty balanced at this time, because poverty is everywhere. It may have been closer to 60 percent black and 40 percent white. I was at the highest custody level when I worked up north. The one thing I knew right away was that being an African American guard was like being on a tightrope. Because I was in the minority and coming from the inner city of Detroit, the administration probably thought that I was there to smuggle stuff in to these guys. But I played sports and went to college up north, so there was some comfort knowing that I had been up there for those years. It was a very challenging time, but I was up for it. There was another corrections officer who came in with me, and they were suspicious of him, because he was a black officer. Prisoners were always looking for ways to gain control, and they knew that they could lie to the administration, especially about a younger, African American officer, and that the officer would be guilty until proven innocent. The prison system was changing in the '80s because there were more black prisoners and more white prisoners and because of the explosion of the prison population, definitely more black guards. The prisons had recently had riots, because the officers didn't want to communicate with the black prisoners. They needed staff who could at least communicate with the prisoners. Where I was at, the white officers were pretty professional. I think it's because there was a military base up north, and a lot of guards came from the military base. Folks from the military were experienced in dealing with different kinds of people. Lifers could see through you, and that could be dangerous if they perceived you as being racist. They have all day to think about doing things to you.

The prison itself looked like a castle. To get a good idea of a prison's layout, just watch the movie *The Shawshank Redemption* (an excellent movie). One thing that struck me right away at Marquette was that the warden, the head man, was living at the prison. This warden was actually the last warden to ever live or have housing directly connected to the prison.

The Marquette Branch Prison housed some of the most dangerous and well-known prisoners in the state of Michigan. I had a guy in there for allegedly authorizing people's heads to be chopped off, probably the last true black gangster to have been locked up in prison. He had judges in his back pocket; he was so powerful that all he wanted to do was use the phone. He was supposedly doing life in prison, but as I transferred back downstate, I remember him coming down on a court on a writ to see a judge for some legal reason; however, administration allowed him to leave for five days—unsupervised. He came back, but that's how powerful he was: he could take a break, see his family, or go on a vacation from prison if he wanted to. I also had a notorious serial rapist from the '60s; it was alleged that six to seven kids came up missing, that he had molested and kill them, but the crime was never solved. I had guys who killed state police and perhaps the most bizarre prisoners—Horse Boy, the child molester and Bigfoot Larry who would snatch a young prisoner into his room for his own self gratifications. I called this the all-star crew, the who's who of Michigan Corrections.

Remember, I was young when I had my first encounter with any prison or prison bars. Prisoners had to be escorted by two corrections officers per one prisoner. They had belly chains around their waists and a black strap connected to the belly chain, and one of the officers held the strap while being escorted to and from the places within the correctional facility.

The first thing that this made me think of was slavery. However, soon I would learn that all of this security—the chains, for instance—was set in place to make sure that the prisoners couldn't hurt each other or the guards. I would spend the next twenty-nine years of my career learning the ins and outs of staying safe while protecting the prisoners from themselves and each other. When I first arrived, the prisoners' conditions seemed inhumane to me because the prisoners had given up their rights to be men. Their behavior made it necessary for them to be controlled, to relinquish their power over their own destinies. The prisoners had to be pawns instead of men; they could no longer be trusted to follow their own moral compasses. They had to be completely controlled by other people for the sake of everyone's safety. Though I spent my days in this environment, with the unique responsibility of bringing my humanity into an inhumane place, I never lost my own clear sense of right and wrong, of why I was there and what my job was.

The lessons I learned from watching my brothers and my father prosper from good, honest work and the discipline I learned from playing basketball all reminded me of who I was when I was confronted by corruption. I would not stand idly by; I would not be stagnant or unchanging; I would not be a pawn. Working in this highly intense environment would make me understand even more of the importance of respect and awareness of your surroundings. As I would come back down state and be with my family during my early days of corrections I would notice that I would stand with my back against the wall whenever I was home on vacations,not knowing that it was from me working in that environment. But because I took on the challenge of getting a comfortable pension after 25 years of working in this setting I was going to fulfill my goal.

Chapter 2

# THE PRISON COMMUNITY

As one of the only African American guards, the vision I had when I started in the prison system was of mostly white people as guards and authorities and mostly black and brown people behind bars or in belly chains and dog straps. Of course, the first thing that came to my mind was slavery. I had never been in an environment like that: I was walking in a housing unit where guys were chained together like animals. Some of these guys would even walk without any towels wrapped around them to the showers, just naked and barefoot, yet still in chains, always with two people walking with them.

This was in the highest custody level, and you'd have guys in their cells able to look at these individuals while they were walking from their cells. So it was an extremely controlled, intense situation, which didn't seem at all like an average, normal, or natural human environment. It was like the walking dead—guys who had no life in their eyes and no shame about appearing indifferent to their lives and the lives of others. After a few months, I got more of an impression of what was going on and why those extreme measures, like dog straps and belly chains, were taken.

I learned quickly that this was all in the best interest of the safety of the staff and of the other prisoners at this level of confinement. If you were sent to this particular institution at this time, you were no boy scout. This is where I would eventually get my feet wet, from a professional standpoint. I would come to understand how a professional corrections officer with a great deal of experience, wisdom, and know-how would control movement and maintain order within these settings.

The correctional staff at Marquette took a no-nonsense approach to their jobs. Correctional officers consistently made it clear to the prisoners that they were in charge. Would they have a little flexibility? Yes. A little sense of humor? Yes. But not to any point that would jeopardize their staff's safety or any policies while doing their jobs. I would go on to experience my first incident that would shape me and force me to understand the seriousness of the career path I had chosen.

I was working in a housing unit called the B block, with two other corrections officers. B block was a housing unit that connected the main population to the prisoners who had been placed in isolated, single-man cells for misbehavior or dangerous actions. It didn't take much for someone to be locked up in solitary confinement: being threatening to an officer or prisoner—any threat of any kind could do it; fighting of any kind, bribery, or contraband; disobeying a direct order—for instance, if an officer ordered a prisoner to go back to their room or area and the prisoner refused; and getting caught with knives or drugs or in a serious fight, they would be locked up for up to a month.

There would be a hearing to determine if the prisoner should go into solitary, where they could be sent from a week to a month. I've seen solitary confinement drive people crazy. Where I worked up north, guys would stay there up to six months because they would keep misbehaving and getting their time in solitary increased. They'd get into solitary and would throw feces or urine on the staff, for example. Some folks would break down eventually, because they have to in order to get out of solitary.

To leave solitary confinement, to get to the general population where prisoners were able to play basketball, chess, run or jog, or walk, they would have to pass through this housing unit: B block. There were three officers, including myself, in charge of guarding this housing unit. The three of us took a lot of pride in keeping the prisoners in B block quiet and under control. We didn't want to hear much, if any, noise or talking.

Now, the prisoners would get angry at times. And at this point, I was still very new to corrections. Remember, I was one of only five African

Americans working at this facility. A lot of eyes of the administrative staff were on me, and the prisoners could perceive this. The fact that I was a minority as a guard could be used as a source of manipulation by the prisoners, who had nothing to do but study the guards and consider what could be used to manipulate us. Many of the prisoners were skilled manipulators, who would work subtly to break you toward their goals (smuggling drugs or other contraband, gaining phone privileges, etc.). When prisoners would act out, we would write tickets, called "petty tickets," to get our point across—that we weren't going to stand for a lot of noise in this housing unit.

One day, a prisoner on the second gallery yelled out, "Hey, send that black, house Negro, up here to my cell; I want to see him!"

He was hollering, and I sensed that there was going to be a problem with this prisoner, but I didn't know what it was gonna be about. I took a cup of coffee with me up the stairs to the second gallery. I had it in a white Styrofoam cup. As I approached the prisoner's cell, he was standing back to the wall, looking at his TV. Like a fool, too confident, I walked directly in front of his cell to speak with him, instead of standing back.

"What do you want?" I asked him.

Now, mind you, my fellow coworkers, two experienced officers, remained downstairs on the main floor, observing me from a distance. They were knowledgeable staff, and looking back, I find it odd that one of them didn't come with me.

After I asked the prisoner what he wanted, he just looked at me.

The next thing I knew, there was a Nolan Ryan fastball or a Justin Verlander fastball of some kind heading right toward my head. I knew it couldn't be a baseball, but it was a white object coming directly at me, and I had no time to get out of the way or to react to this situation.

What saved me were the cell bars, which were vertical and horizontal on his room. Some clear liquid came out of the object as it hit the bars; it was made of glass. It sounded like a bottle breaking as it hit the cell bars, and some kind of liquid fell on me.

I immediately threw my cup of coffee at the prisoner. He was surprised, and I was too. I then went down the stairs and back to the desk area, where my coworkers looked me over, and we had some bumbling fun with the situation. The prisoner was written up and put back into the other units of confinement, which he didn't mind since he wasn't going anywhere—he was here for life.

I might have joked with my fellow coworkers about the incident, but when I got home to my apartment that night, I realized the seriousness and danger that existed within this institution. I could've easily had my face rearranged, an eye out, or my nose broken if the object that was thrown had not hit that cell bar. I knew then how important it was to remain professional and straightforward with the dangerous criminals in my charge.

A few prisoners would tell me during the course of my time working in this unit, B block, "Son, you need to be your own man (correctional officer); don't follow others' footsteps, especially those who are not somewhat flexible." By this, they meant officers who didn't listen to the prisoners' grievances. I kind of shrugged off all this advice at the time. But I would learn the importance of listening and being fair very quickly.

I did see some neglect among other guards—not a lot, because again at that level it was very dangerous to play that type of game. The guards understood that they were guarding very dangerous prisoners. During my twenty-nine years, there were at least two guards killed in the Michigan Department of Corrections. A woman was killed around the time I first started. She was an inexperienced guard in a big prison downstate; she was mainly there to observe what was going on. She was still learning and didn't know how dangerous prisoners could be. This officer was lured into an area where she was raped and killed. They rounded up seven or eight prisoners and fingerprinted one prisoner, who was already doing life. He went to court for added time, but ultimately there was nothing more to do to him.

Another officer who was allegedly mishandling the prisoners was also killed. He was allegedly disciplining prisoners with unnecessary harshness and severity, including mistreatment and abuse. He was stabbed and killed by one of the prisoners he had abused. A third guard was almost killed by a prisoner who had just six months left on his sentence. While working on a road crew, this prisoner beat the officer severely, and the officer nearly died.

My own experience of the prisoner's fastball shaped me and awakened me to the professional approach I had to take while working in this environment, and it served me well. I would go on to respect others and to be respected while doing my job. I would go on to have a very valuable and positive experience while working in Marquette for two years, due to the help and respect of two captains who worked up there at the time.

The day-shift captain and the second-shift captain were very professional. They each had a calm demeanor, as individuals and in the workplace. One day, about six months on the job, we would go over to a part of the prison that housed isolated inmates. These prisoners were locked down for twenty-four hours per day; they had no officer communication, no physical contact with anyone, and were only let out from a pane inside the control center.

Around 10:30 p.m., most nights, the two captains from the day shift and the afternoon shift and about thirteen other officers went to the control center area to play basketball. This was necessary to relieve stress and provided a basic workout. I had the privilege of having both the day captain and the night captain on my team of five players. I was twenty-two years old, and they both had to be about forty-five years old. They wore knee wraps, and I thought I could smell Ben-Gay on them. I spoon-fed them, passing behind the back and making other passes for open jump shots because the guys had to double-team me. Remember, I had played some college ball and was a pretty good high-school basketball player. We would win several games that night and from that point on, my working assignments and stay at Marquette were pretty good.

I would go on to work for the next eight years in the lowest custody level of the prison system, in what's called a halfway house setting, where prisoners were called residents. It was a residential setting, where they could go out and find a job. They would get five hours out to find a job, from 8:00 a.m. to 1:00 p.m., Monday through Friday, and ten hours on the weekends, Saturday and Sunday from 8:00 a.m. to 6:00 p.m. If they didn't come back at the appropriate time, they could and would be sent back to a correctional facility.

I enjoyed working in this setting due to the responses the staff would get from the families of the residents. They would call us and thank us for helping their loved ones stay on the straight and narrow path of finding and maintaining employment. Some of them would say, "We've never seen him with a job, and his kids especially love it." There's something to be said for the importance of young children having a stable, powerful role model; they need to see their fathers working to try and improve their lives. If the child sees this, he'll try to respond by doing the same himself.

There were a lot of young men in prison, filled with testosterone, ready and eager to fight with each other or anyone. There were all types of gangs; there was a Christian gang, a Muslim gang, a skinhead gang—prisoners join these gangs to survive, for community and support. The Christian gang, for example, really did study the bible and try to get right with themselves. They had services, and if you were a part of it, the gang was a source of protection. You also had to abide by certain rules. The Christians, for example, didn't like their members to playing cards or gamble. The Muslim gangs—there were a couple different groups: Muslims, Nation of Islam, who were well-disciplined Muslims with a lot of respect for others. They acted respectful and professional. There were also other Muslim groups who were into drug trafficking, like the skinhead group, or Aryan Nation. These bigger gangs are interconnected with each other across the prison system, so if there's something they want to get (e.g., cigarettes), they could get it.

While working in a correctional setting, I started to understand the communities that formed there and why they were so important. What I mean by this is that there are structural organizations of prisoners, which we call gangs but which almost anyone inside a prison would want to affiliate themselves with in order to survive. The organization would educate you on prison and life. The streets have no structure, and once guys are in prison, they don't know how to survive. Do you have to join a gang to survive in prison? No. But can anyone just be on their own without any consequences? No. I'd give you a 10 percent chance of survival. There are some who make it through on their own, but if they are trying to hustle (through play cards, betting on sporting events, selling items, etc.), they'll be immediately shut down by the gang whose business they're threatening. You would probably not last very long this way, and soon you'd find yourself calling Mom, Dad, Girlfriend, Uncle, Auntie, Grandmother, or Grandfather to send you some money so that you could pay money to get various threats off your back. If people knew you were in a gang or organization, they wouldn't mess with you. I wouldn't advise any of my loved ones to chance doing prison time without a group of people watching out for them.

A lot of the prisoners joined these organizations to find themselves. Each group had a certain amount of intrigue. I don't believe they were principally supporting anger toward each other or anyone; their agendas were different, but they mainly functioned to support their members, not to cause harm to outsiders. All these organizations are interconnected; meaning that they would and will continue to come together for common causes, especially contraband smuggling (cigarettes, marijuana, heroin, pills, etc.), which they see as benefiting everyone in the environment.

Younger prisoners would soon learn the ropes and decide which organization was the best for them. It would only be one or two organizations that cause any real problems. For the most part, guys were trying to really do their best to find out who and what their purpose in life was. Most prisoners were lost in an identity crisis, and these communities gave them an identity. One thing that the younger prisoner would pick up pretty fast was the fact that the older, more established prisoners did not like a lot of drama or attention directed toward them. Attention brings correctional staff snooping around, possibly finding information that otherwise would not have been found, such as large quantities of store items (soap, toothpaste, candy, tobacco, food, all of which was controlled).

If a young person caused these items to be confiscated due to their emotional tantrum, they'd be calling home to Mom, Dad, Uncle, Aunt, Grandparent, or Girlfriend for some money to help bail them out of a very dangerous situation, because you may have a few different organizations involved in these illegal actions. Some of these things that go on inside the prison setting should be available as information for young, hardheaded non prisoner type of individuals who are out on the streets believing that they can handle themselves OK if they get to this level of lockup. They're fooling themselves. All that talk about "my homeboy has my back—Timothy and Ronnie from the neighborhood or township or rural community," are nothing but ghost tales when Bigfoot Larry, who runs the yard, says, "Hey, your homeboy owes me, and I'll be collecting tonight; I don't want to see you around." Bigfoot Larry is six feet five, 270 lbs., strong as an ox, and in for life. What do you think your homeboy or township boy or rural community boy is going to do to Bigfoot Larry?" Believe me it was not going to be pretty".

As I grew in experience at the prison, I became more and more convinced that rehabilitation should be the focus of prison life. The prisoners respected and trusted me. They saw the way I carried myself, that I was positive and straightforward and truthful with them. I spoke often with them about how they should get their lives in order. I would ask them if they had any kids out there, and they'd say yeah, and it didn't matter what nationality, I got respect from a lot of the guys.

I did run across guys who said they didn't do it, but because of the pressures of the communities, they took the rap. Taking the rap for your best buddy was fairly common, but there were hardly ever men taking the rap for women. I've known a lot of women locked up for taking the rap for their man, but I've never heard of the reverse. Every now and then, a guy would admit that they'd let a woman take the rap for them but only once in a while. It depended on how selfish the guy was. Most prisoners were very selfish individuals, putting their families in bad situations just to pursue their own ends. In women's prisons, it was very common to find women who took the blame for their guys. They'd be in a car with their man who was selling drugs and get pulled over, and the man would actually let the woman take the blame for the drugs or guns in the car.

But I have seen in my journey working at these centers that these programs were really a very positive part of these men's lives, because these guys had to go out and find jobs and be with their families. A lot of guys really wanted to do the right thing, but they had no guidance. Corrections officers can really become role models to these guys, if they perform their jobs with respect and professionalism.

A positive, supportive relationship between correctional officers and prisoners, or residents, makes it more difficult for prisoners to manipulate guards. Manipulative prisoners thrive on divisiveness; they try to get one or two staff members to see a situation their way, which then allows them to spin them (manipulate them, corrupt them). Ultimately, the goal of the prisoners was to bring in more contraband.

You might wonder how corrections officers would come to be manipulated or bribed by prisoners. It would start out small. Some officers would do little things for prisoners because of neighborhood ties; black or white, hometown ties are still strong, even if you end up on different sides of the jail bars. If officers don't separate their professional lives from their personal lives and histories, these relationships can be dangerously manipulated. As soon as you get personal and the prisoner finds out when you're up or when you're down and not feeling good, to a female guard he'll say something like, "If I was your man, I'd drink your bathwater," and depending on how she reacts, he knows what he can get away with. She's supposed to threaten to write him up, but if she doesn't, it opens the door for him to go further. The next thing you know, he's asking for toothpaste, gum, and then a cell phone. Now the pressure's on you, and you did it before; if you don't do it, he'll tell the authorities, so you say, "OK, I'll do it one more time..." Most of it is manipulation, but there are some people who get involved for money as well.

Because of my experience up north, being at the prison where you wouldn't dare get close to a prisoner, because it was so high security among the lifers, I quickly understood the consequences of bending the rules around the prison. Working there for three years was like working five years anywhere else. I'd get subtly asked for a stick of gum, but I'd quickly squash that. I would clearly let it be understood that I would tell, that I would report it. So prisoners wouldn't even waste time trying to manipulate me. You want to be flexible to keep your area safe and let them know you are flexible while being fair; for instance, a prisoner may have an abundance of food that he shouldn't have, but by you not taking that food, you're being flexible. Because he may not have the financial means to get stuff from the store, you can let him have his extra food, and that goes a long way. Or for instance, if you ran a housing unit and if the guys came off the yard, you didn't want anybody to be drunk, but if you could see in their eyes that they're a little high or something, but you know he's just going to fall asleep, he's not being a problem. Now, you may make him drop urine tomorrow, but whatever he does out on the yard, if it's not making a problem, you can be flexible. I tried to make a distinction between dangerous situations and problems verses rule breaking, which was human. With simple rule violations, I would just talk to the guy about it and not humiliate or embarrass him. I'd say, "Hey, just don't do it again," verses writing him up. If I was flexible, then prisoners would eventually come to me if they knew that something dangerous was going on. Most prisoners want comfort and safety. If you're flexible, they'll trust you with things that are more serious.

Male guards were vulnerable to manipulation, but female guards were also uniquely vulnerable.

A lot of young women who had kids and careers were damaged tremendously by working in this environment. I knew of at least thirty-five women who lost their jobs due to being manipulated by prisoners. Often these women were hardworking single mothers, and they were lonely. Loneliness, not having a man at home, looking for love in the wrong places, and the attraction of a dangerous romance with a prisoner—all these factors contributed to a high rate of female staff falling in love with prisoners. There was training about not being manipulated, but when you're constantly around people, and you let your guard down, you can get too comfortable.

The same thing would happen to men but not through romance. With male guards, prisoners would start out by getting into conversations about sports or other things they had in common. Then they would make harmless bets about sports games, such as betting push-ups. Betting push-ups would escalate to betting a candy bar out of the vending machine. As that officer got closer and closer to the prisoner and as the prisoner reeled him closer, they would bet a pack of cigarettes; then they'd have the officer bringing in some contraband; then they'd offer to pay to bring in more serious things.

One guard I worked with definitely followed this progression. The prisoner started off betting the guard push-ups on games, then the next thing was to buy some chips out of the vending machine, then the prisoner got comfortable enough to tell the officer that he could give him money to bring in some weed, which piqued the interest of the officer, and he said he would do it. The guard took $500 from the prisoner but didn't bring him the drugs. The prisoner ended up beating him up right in the housing unit.

When the state police came to investigate the beating, the prisoner tried to blackmail them too. They were interrogating the prisoner about what happened, and instead of feeling threatened by their presence, the prisoner demanded that they produce the marijuana that he felt he had purchased.

"If you don't get back my money or get me my weed," he said to them, "I'll beat your asses!"

The state police weren't interested in any of this, and that corrections officer got fired. Yet there was little that could be done to the prisoner.

Sometimes I would ask myself, "Is this really happening? How can these prisoners feel so unafraid and entitled?" I realized eventually that it was complicated. Not only did many of these lifers have nothing to lose, because they were already serving impossible sentences, but they'd also spent a lot of time inside, and they were very aware that they could control and manipulate staff through fear. They were also aware that every member of the staff was potentially corruptible, and there were no real consequences for trying to bribe officers. These hardened lifers weren't afraid of solitary and were willing to take the risk for the possibility of getting drugs, money, cell phones or other contraband. All this helped me to realize that a system focused on punishment rather than rehabilitation is going to keep perpetuating this kind of bad behavior. If prisoners have no reason to improve their behavior, they won't be inspired to change.

I would always try to intervene if I saw anything. The problem with female officers is, by the time you recognize it, they're in a trance, and no matter what you say, he's gotten into their head, so nothing can be done until it crashes. Men would have strong emotional connections based on where they were from.

Additionally, I learned that it may not be the prisoner who is talking to the guard who's doing the actual manipulating. When a powerful, tough guy in the prison sees another prisoner connecting with a guard, the tough guy will coerce that prisoner into using the connection. Then once the doors open, they'll pressure the officer together to do whatever they want. Officers start off small and can end up passing files or weapons into the very prison system they are supposed to be guarding.

A female kitchen worker once fell in love with a prisoner who worked in the kitchen with her, and she helped him escape through a food cart that was going to the trash bin.

Corrections had always been a good old boys club. In the eighties and nineties, the only people who got promoted, even among the high administrative staff, were screw ups. Anyone who had two or three disciplinary packets could get promoted—not every single promotion, but most promotions came that way.

In 2009 there were two individuals working at the Mound Correctional Facility who were being promoted more due to their inaction and their ability to get into trouble than their skills as corrections officers. These two individuals, whom I'll describe more later, rose to prominent positions within the correctional facility. These men were very influential and could get you fired in a heartbeat or even arrested for actions done on state prison property. These two would walk around as if they were the Taliban, ISIS, the Gestapo, or the KGB, ready to dole out the ultimate punishment for the slightest infraction.

The staff at Mound Correctional Facility were a family who stuck together, and before long those individuals were removed from their duties as administrators at Mound and moved to another correctional facility—Ryan Correctional Facility—which was just next door, over the hill. You may wonder why two administrators would be removed from one correctional facility and be escorted over to another facility without being demoted. This is puzzling to me as well. But one thing I'm sure of, it was because of their own actions, not that of the majority of the correctional staff at Mound. Mound staff did not clap or applaud when these individuals were removed from the facility. Within a few months, we would get a new group of young correctional officers at Mound Correctional Facility.

The young staff at Mound were up to the task, and brought a tremendously strong group of correctional officers together, and for a time I witnessed very little corruption. Corrections was going through a growing process at this time. More facilities were popping up due to the drug trafficking of the late eighties and early nineties. The younger staff were more educated, and they were coming to the department with two or three years of college, even college degrees, so they had to be reined in a little. When I came into corrections, it was like we were told, "You have to do it this way, period." The younger, new corrections officers would always ask, "Why? Why not this other way?" They were very much engaged with what was going on and always wanted to improve—though sometimes they wanted to improve in areas that I don't think the department actually agreed with.

We had been through a number of administrative staff over a six-year period, and they always seemed to keep the facility running smoothly. We once had a regional administrator come to our facility to find out what we were doing that other correctional facilities could emulate. We did not have a large number of assaults, and our problems were minimal. This was so important to the department up in Lansing, that there was not a lot of drama at our institution, especially after those two individuals were removed.

I believe that our success was due in part to the family atmosphere brought about by the senior staff, who had been at other facilities (Jackson Prison, Huron Valley, Scott's, and Western Wayne). These experienced officers knew the importance of togetherness as correctional staff. These senior staff members had seen and been around correctional staff who had been assaulted, stabbed, and even murdered—may they rest in peace. Surviving all of this brought about unity among the staff. We understood the highs and lows that went with the job and always tried to stay positive and have positive interactions away from the facilities, including picnics, cabaret functions, and bowling outings. The administrators would join in these gatherings as well, which made for a unique lesson in accountability by all the staff at this facility. Seeing each other outside of the negative environment, where we spent most of our time, was necessary for us to build up positive communication between staff and administration. This positive community contact built up trust so that people could communicate honestly when there were problems.

This culture of community and camaraderie made everyone want to come to work and do their best on a daily basis. There were some funny moments in corrections around this time, things that made me scratch my head and say, "What the hell? Did this really happen in a prison?"

One such incident happened on Thanksgiving Day, 2010. There were two housing units connected by a walkway we called the "bowtie area." There were two levels in each housing unit: twenty-four cells in the upper level housing forty-eight men and twenty-four cells in the lower level housing forty-eight men, with a total of ninety-six beds in one housing unit. The prisoners from one housing unit were out of the unit, eating, and the prisoners I was in charge of, from the other housing unit, were sitting around playing cards and watching football in the day rooms, like so many Americans do on Thanksgiving. It was around 1:00 p.m.; it was quiet. The water fountain in my unit was broken, so I asked Officer Bill, who was in charge of the other prisoners, to watch over my prisoners while I went over to his side to get a drink of water. He agreed, and we switched places so that I could get a drink.

While I was still standing at the fountain, I heard a lot of cheering going on from across the bowtie, in my housing unit. It was quiet where I was because Bill's prisoners were eating in the cafeteria. I walked toward the television to see what the commotion was, thinking that one of the teams playing had scored a big touchdown or something. The football play on TV was just someone running out of bounds with the football, so I thought, "Hmm, that's strange, all that cheering for a guy running out of bounds with the football..."

That's when I looked back through the bowtie hallway area of my unit and saw prisoners standing up, cheering, "Go, go, go, go!" I approached my side of the unit, but I did not see the corrections officer, Bill, anywhere.

Then I looked up to the upper level of the unit, and there he was. He was standing on a table in the hallway, pop-locking. And then he started to break dance. Mind you, this is happening in real time, with ninety-six prisoners looking on, cheering, "Go, go, go, go!"

As I'm observing all this, I noticed he didn't have his utility belt on (which contained his handcuffs and accessories). It was on the table up there with him. I remember the music being the disco song, "Electric Kingdom," a song that was popular to pop-lock and break dance to in the eighties and nineties. After pop-locking and break dancing for about a minute, Bill jumped to the floor and did what looked like the snake or the worm—hell, I didn't know what he was doing!

Suddenly there was a popping sound, and Bill stopped dancing. He had popped his back; he grabbed his utility belt and painfully come down the stairs toward me. I asked him, "What the hell came over you?"

He looked sheepish, and said, "I was just in a zone."

I said, "In a zone?"

"Yeah, I had won fourth place in a dance-off when I was in high school."

"Is that so?" I asked, looking pointedly toward his injured back.

"There's a YouTube video of me, too, called Hillbilly Break Dancer."

This made us both laugh. Bill hadn't been to high school for twenty-two years; he was at least forty years old. He would make it to work for two more days, painfully sitting in a chair at his unit desk. After those two days, we didn't see Bill for five more months. He had slipped a disc in his back and required surgery. Fourth place in a dance-off, huh? Maybe twenty years earlier!

The guards worked hard and needed every paycheck. One year, I had to work on New Year's Day. I had to walk past the chow hall(dining), and I saw two of my coworkers, who were clearly the worse for wear. They had clearly been partying the night before. One white and one black, they were sitting, eating waffles and sausages in the break room, looking hungover. It wasn't unusual for the corrections staff to eat the same food that the prisoners ate, because state workers helped the prisoners in preparing the food. I could see Warren, the Caucasian, and Tad, the African American, eating as usual.

When I opened the door to the health-care area, where I was assigned to work that day, I could see that a few officers had a rough night on New Year's Eve, the night before. One of them was leaning back in the chair, with sunglasses on, snoring, and another was leaning forward, trying to hang in there. A third officer was right by the elevator, leading to the upstairs area where we housed the isolated prisoners. Now, there are just two bathroom areas in the lower floor where all of these hungover individuals were scattered, recovering from the holiday.

It was my job to serve food to the prisoners in isolation. I had just gotten the food on a cart, when I had to pass the three corrections officers who were struggling to even begin their assignments. I took the cart onto the elevator and went to the second floor—to the segregation unit. At the time, there were roughly eight prisoners in the unit, with one officer stationed there to guard them. As I proceeded to open their slots and give them their eggs, waffles, and syrup, I noticed that I needed more supplies from my cart, which I had left by the elevator. I headed back and opened the door to the main hallway. Looking back through the hallway toward the elevator, I saw what I can only describe as a long line of something that looked like the chili you'd get on your Coney Island hot dog. Except that this chili had a horrible smell to it. There was a long line of this foul stuff, from the elevator to the staff bathroom.

I immediately asked the staff member watching the segregation unit to look into the hallway and tell me what he saw and what he smelled.

He looked at me, bewildered and puzzled, and then, looking out into the hall, he just shook his head.

By this time, we both heard some keys jingling in the bathroom and water running.

I went to check the food cart that I brought up, to make absolutely sure that this "chili" wasn't coming from my cart. It definitely wasn't.

At that point I changed my focus to going back downstairs to find those three individuals who had been so obviously hungover in their chairs. The segregation officer just went back to his chair, shaking his head.

To get to the elevator, I had to walk along about fifteen feet of this foul smelling "chili." I opened the elevator door and took a step toward getting on, and I damn near threw up.

What I saw on the elevator looked like a scene from the old *Psycho* movie, where the lady was stabbed and stained the bathroom with blood. But this wasn't blood; this was what looked like chocolate pudding, smeared all down the elevator wall and in a puddle on the carpeted floor.

After preventing myself from vomiting somehow, I stepped back and said, "What the hell!"

I went down the back stairwell to see which one of those three individuals had just made this disaster of the elevator and the upstairs.

But all three individuals were still there; one leaning back in his sunglasses, one slumped over on a bench, and one sitting in the office, leaning back by the elevator that led upstairs.

At this point I asked them, "Who went up the elevator to the bathroom upstairs? It's a disaster!"

The officer on the bench sat up, burping, and said, "I just let Tad up there; he was holding one of his pant legs, and he asked me to hurry up, and let him up the elevator."

Well, Tad didn't make it to his destination in time. I had all these guys take a look into the elevator, and you know what came next. Their stomachs got uneasy too.

I felt bad for Tad, because he was a hardworking man. We knew he was in the bathroom washing his pants in the sink, because we could hear the water running. I felt bad for the prison porter, who had to clean up that mess. He wasn't feeling it either. A few other staff came to the area to survey the scene, and a discussion started about how to help Tad. Some suggested that we give him a prison jumpsuit, and walk him through the sally port to his car. Another said, "Let him take a shower; we can put his clothes in the dryer." Everyone was hungover, and none of these ideas were put into action.

Tad came out of the bathroom area after everyone had cleared out and gone back to work. He proceeded to his assignment, which was working the visiting room that day. Everyone wondered why he wouldn't just go home after such an unfortunate experience. But Tad said that he didn't want to lose his overtime holiday pay. The poor guy had to work the visiting room for prisoners and family members, even though he still bore the faint smell of that morning's foul disaster.

At this time, I was just two or three years away from retiring. I thought I had seen enough in corrections to last me a lifetime. I had been the Corrections Officer of the Year for my region in 1995, which gave me the chance to mingle with the warden and the director in Lansing, at the award ceremonies. I had a stellar reputation, with coworkers and prisoners alike, for being professional, respectful, and accountable. I always tried to be positive and consistent in my daily duties and job performance.

The younger prisoners I encountered during my career as a correctional officer would frequently come to me for positive direction or advice. They saw the way I conducted myself with the other, older prisoners as well as the other correctional staff. I guess they considered me to be fair in my assessments and judgments of prisoners and others. They knew I would be consistent, straightforward, and truthful. I was respected by all the different nationalities in prison, black, white, Hispanic, Indian—yes, Indian, they were locked up too!

I would ask honest questions and try to get honest answers. I've even asked a question to a lifer who was in for murder. I didn't like to take too much time to talk to prisoners, especially lifers, who were especially dangerous.

"Could you tell me the truth?" I asked, "Do you see the person that you murdered? How does that affect you?"

"Yeah, I do," he said, "That's why I can't sleep at night."

And that let me know he had a conscience—a conscience that was kicking him in the butt. I knew that most of these guys hadn't really gotten away with what they had done, even if they seemed to pass their time with some contentment.

I also asked prisoners to tell me about other officers. An officer can't play on the side and still try to do his job. They would let me know about those things. I wouldn't hold a conversation for too long. Prisoners want you to entertain them; they'll do things to make themselves stand out, like roll their pants legs up, wear pants inside out, anything to be different. There are even some prisoners who would set their sleep patterns around, just to be different. Some people would do anything to break up that sameness of life in the prison.

I had the patience to listen and give feedback about what I thought each individual prisoner needed to do. For instance, some young men would come to me and open up about criminal cases or their family history. I would always ask, first, if they had any kids. Next, I would ask if they had a girlfriend or wife.

Without a doubt, the most influential motivation for a man to get out of prison was the woman in his life. Now, as I walk around, in charge of this housing unit, which is about ninety-six guys, I'd find nearly every guy would get up as early as they could and call his girlfriend. And once in a while you would hear a guy ask, "Hey, what's all that moaning I hear in the background?" It was clear that a lot of their girls weren't waiting for them to get out. I would tell them that unless they got themselves together, they wouldn't just lose their freedom, they'd lose their girlfriends too. I'd say to them, "If that woman told you she's done with you if you break the law, would you change?" And they'd say, "Yeah."

I surveyed at least two hundred prisoners, asking them if they would stop their criminal activity for the sake of the women in their lives. At least 85 percent of them said they would seriously consider it if the woman remained devoted to them. If she wanted to see any results, she had to stay firm and strong in her decision to cut off the relationship if the man went back to crime. But most young and older women I saw did not stand strong in this decision. They would wonder why their man, their boo, their soul mate, would not follow through on his promise to get out of crime, yet they would not remain firm in their threat to leave him if he didn't. If they would, they'd see a dramatic change in the morality of these individuals. I was able to see firsthand that many of the paroled guys did follow through with their women, learning to work hard and hold down whatever job, pay whatever bills, and take care of whatever households they created.

I saw many men lose the women in their lives due to being in prison and get so involved in the streets that they lost their focus on what's really important: take care of their women, take care of their families, work hard, and be responsible for their own actions. I would ask them, "Why would you let your homeboy or buddy influence you to do something so stupid that you would consider being out of the life of that woman you love so dearly? Maybe he wants what you have, and you're in the way, and you don't even see it." Like the legendary O Jays music group saying in the seventies, "They Smile in Your Face" (but steal your girl behind your back). He might be trying to raise your kid or kids and date or marry your girl or wife. He might really want you to get out of the picture. These are examples of the kind of prison mentality that crept into not just the black communities but all the other communities as well. Whether they are men or women, prisoners learn to play these mental games.

Because I was straightforward and honest with them, the younger prisoners would occasionally ask me questions. They'd ask me about choices that I made, and they would even ask me for my honest assessment of what had gotten them into trouble and how to change their path toward a more positive direction. I would sometimes hear, "I wish you were my uncle, father, or brother…then maybe I wouldn't be in this position." This did not just come from the black prisoners; again, I was able to talk and communicate with all the different races of men under my charge. This initially surprised some of the white prisoners, but they said that they could trust me because of my actions. I wouldn't allow race to determine how I did my job one way or the other. Some guys would act like I should favor them because they were black or because they were from the inner city, as I was. But I wouldn't allow anyone to think I was favoring anyone. I always took the approach that we are all men, and we were going to behave as men. And if we don't behave as men, if we behave like animals, there are consequences to that. I ran housing units for the most part, so I would never be drawn into any kind of favoritism, and all the guys truly respected that.

I lived in the Upper Peninsula for four years and went to school with people from different parts of Michigan. So I was familiar with different kinds of people and their views. Basically, there were some basic commonalities;

for instance, parents want to see their kids in a positive light. All parents want to see their kids grow up and be somewhat successful, have a stable home, be able to have a family, and find satisfying work. Parents want their children to be able to go out on their own and be independent. All ethnicities of people can know right from wrong, can respect others, and can become decent, law-abiding citizens. We all have those abilities inside of us, those common values with which we can relate to each other. No one wants to see their loved one imprisoned in this kind of setting, if they can help it. All ethnicities have common core values that we strive toward and to be. If more of us were truthful in our approach to the younger generation, we might be able to change their directions in a positive way.

Once most prisoners reach seven to eight years of incarceration, they begin to mature. Young men start to realize all the damage they've done to themselves, their families, and their communities. Some of them will become very remorseful and try their best to give back to their communities in a way that could make up for some of the negative things they have done. One of the most successful programs I observed within the prison was the Youth Deterrent Program. With this program, religious leaders and community activist groups brought young, at-risk males from different walks of life to the prison, and then a group of prisoners would speak to the kids. They would open up about their experiences as young men and what led them to be incarcerated. The prisoners would not hold back their feelings, as far as their upbringing, education, downfall, peer pressure, and eventually why they chose to speak that day. This program was about listening and understanding and providing input and serious feedback to at-risk youth, rather than scaring them. The Scared Straight Program tried to frighten at-risk youth into staying in school and staying off the street. However, that program neglected to acknowledge that the motivations for youth to engage in crime and to underperform in school were often brought on by fear, especially fear of authority, violence, and poverty. The Youth Deterrent Program engaged youth not by scaring them but by telling them the truth.

Three guys, named 2-X, Woody, and Spoon, ran the Youth Deterrent Program while I was there. 2-X, Woody, and Spoon were all doing a long time in jail, for armed robbery and selling drugs, possibly even manslaughter. These men told the truth about their lives to the teens who came to listen. These inmates had been young when they came in, and you could see the change in them and the maturity that they were willing to open themselves up to at-risk kids, white or black, and give them a better chance for improving their lives. They'd tell the stories of their crimes and give explanations, taking responsibility for their mistakes. This wasn't preachers or mothers telling their sons to behave; it was hardened criminals opening up to the younger versions of themselves. These men took off their tough-guy masks and set aside their pride in order to make a difference to the next generation. I wouldn't say anything to them, but they knew I appreciated what they did. They were doing a tremendous job and getting recognized in the papers for their work. Soon, we had kids visiting from Toledo, Kalamazoo, Pontiac, and other metropolitan communities in the Detroit area.

2-X, Woody, and Spoon were focused on talking to the guys and opening up to them, not threatening them. Some people are used to threats, but many people are in there in the first place because of threats and mistreatment, and if you come out of that environment, threats don't help you. 2-X, Woody, and Spoon worked with eight or so other older guys, who ran this program, who were sincere about trying to connect with younger prisoners, to share the wisdom they had learned after spending much of their lives behind bars.

These prisoners weren't required to reach out and speak to these kids nor did they get rewarded for doing it. But they felt an obligation to try and change other young men's lives so that this younger generation could be helped to avoid mistakes. These men did not receive any incentives for participating in this program, even though I believe it should have been evidence that they were rehabilitated and ready to give back positively to their communities, even from within the prison. Even though these prisoners showed signs of initiative and rehabilitation, there was nothing in place in the system to acknowledge this.

At this time, back in the '90s, the War on Drugs and mandatory minimums were crowding prisons with men who had double or triple life sentences. Also at this time, states started closing mental-health facilities and started lumping people into the prison settings where they should have never been.

In my years of correctional service, the main thing that I learned was that instead of rehabilitating prisoners, most administrative staff were more concerned with their own egos, with inflating themselves as individuals, with making themselves feel important by running the prison like their own personal empire. These men were tyrants who preyed on the weak and defenseless, who were more interested in going on their own power trips, controlling their staff or whoever was beneath them, instead of considering themselves as part of a community of rehabilitation or *correction*.

For many important figures, correctional work was not about helping others, it was a puppet show, a display of power to make them feel better about themselves by dominating and controlling others. This goes back to the metaphor of the chess game; while some of us were content to do our work, to serve and protect the prisoners in our charge, others were more interested in playing the game.

## Chapter 3
# THE KING, THE QUEEN, AND THE BISHOP

The two most corrupt officers I ever encountered exemplified this fact that some of the most powerful people in corrections were not working in this field to rehabilitate or correct prisoners but were working in the system for their own gain. This is where I saw a real problem with the commercialization of prisons and the fact that prisons can be so profitable. When dishonest men are in positions of power, they can exploit the fact that their fellow men are locked up just to make a few extra dollars or make themselves feel more powerful.

This makes a game out of men's lives—men who have one lifetime to recover from their mistakes and try to figure out how to contribute to society. If their only models inside the prison walls are corrupt officials who are committing crimes themselves and not being punished, why would any prisoner be motivated to become honest or follow the law? Corruption inside a prison just convinces prisoners that there is no point in trying to follow the law or improve their lives. If they see corrections officers getting away with abuses, it's confirmed for them that their mistake wasn't committing the crime; it was getting caught for the crime.

Remember, there were two abusive individuals who were removed from Mound Correctional Facility for their corrupt behavior—namely, the harassment, even sexual harassment, of their employees and prisoners. These individuals were not removed from the prison system but merely transferred next door to Ryan Correctional Facility, which was just a few miles away. These two administrators were Alec and Wayman. Now, if you knew there was corruption and abuse happening and you wanted to stop it, you would fire the individuals responsible. But the Michigan Department of Corrections merely moved these two administrators, rather than firing them. This says to me that the two individuals must have had some dirt on folks even higher up than they were, because they were being protected.

Alec was a deputy warden, while Wayman was an inspector. For the most part in Michigan, the deputy warden really ran the prison, and the second most important person was the inspector. The inspector was the person in charge of bringing in the actual state police. Since the inspector was the contact person between the state police and the prison, he decided which prison transgressions would be reported to authorities beyond the prison walls and whom the police would come down on. In the game of chess that dominated the prison facility, Inspector Wayman would be the most powerful piece, the queen, while Deputy Warden Alec would be another powerful piece, a bishop, who can cross the whole board at once if he needs to.

These two controlled the warden of Ryan, who, like the king in the chess game, seemed to have no real power even though he was supposed to be in charge. The warden had the power to discipline the staff, but this particular warden had no camaraderie whatsoever with his staff. Whatever they brought to him, he would find them guilty before any kind of investigation. He wouldn't even ask questions or consider anyone's point of view besides the person making the accusation. Just imagine, a facility that's supposed to be within the justice system operating like a dictatorship.

No honest or fair staff member would bring any accusation to this man, if they knew that there was no chance of there being a fair trial, so to speak. Likewise, people who were more interested in their own agendas than fairness were happy and comfortable abusing the situation. This turned all the tables upside down, and those who were seeking to serve and protect the prisoners and other staff had to live in fear of those who were willing to abuse the system. I believe that these conditions were what brought about such a crazy, hostile working environment, the likes of which I had never seen in all my years working in the prison. If you were suspected of anything, you were automatically guilty. A lot of people were fired, so everyone was nervous and mistrustful, so they really couldn't do their jobs. The warden-king ruled with an iron fist and only listened to Alec and Wayman.

When Alec and Wayman were placed at the Ryan Correctional Facility, retaining their same titles, the Ryan Facility caught the blues. Now, with the help of the warden-king who was already in place there, the Ryan Facility became like a Communist regime. We will call it a "regime" because it was corrupt in nature and because the staff were terrified, scared, afraid to do the jobs they were hired to do. In a climate of fear, no one can trust anyone else to respond properly to a situation.

Remember, this was a correction facility, a place where people were supposed to be able to improve themselves while paying their debt to society. This became impossible when the people who were supposed to enforce the law and the rules were more interested in manipulating the rules for their own gain. The regime's prison facility had become known among the staff as "the twelve years of slavery," as a joke based on the movie that had just come out.

Sexual harassment, hostility in the work environment, and quid pro quo were prevalent. To survive in this context, people had to know what side to be on. This meant that now staff and administrators had to manipulate each other to figure out who was on which side and just to survive in this work environment. Supervisors, captains, sergeant, lieutenants, counselors, and other supportive staff knew what side of the pendulum the power swung on. Everyone knew that the three people in charge were corrupt, and everyone had to make a choice about how to engage with them. Some of us just kept our heads low and hoped that their sins would out them. Others were eager to follow suit, to follow in the steps of their supervisors and try to profit.

A lot of lives were changed due to this hostile environment. No one could get a fair disciplinary conference. If you were on the wrong side of the regime, you'd be found guilty of any disciplinary action before you even got a chance to defend yourself. If you were willing to turn a blind eye, to play along, or to incriminate yourself by participating in the corruption, then you were still afraid of getting caught. No one was treated fairly; everyone was guilty. This lead to a depressing environment for the staff who worked at the facility, so morale was terribly low.

The regime took great pleasure in the intimidation they used and the stronghold they had over the staff of correctional officers. The warden-king, Wayman (the queen), and Alec (the bishop) made their power known to the staff whenever they got a chance. The warden and other individuals who could've put a stop to all this allowed Wayman and Alec to rule with a level of power that was unwarranted and unnecessary to get the job done. Their display of power was not about improving the lives of prisoners through proper programs and role models; it was about what they called "getting even." This meant getting even with the prisoners for what they had done to society, as if these individuals were capable of doling out justice themselves.

Then the staff at Mound Correctional Facility got some extremely bad news: the warden who was running both Ryan and Mound Correctional Facilities had the authority too close one or the other facility. You may be able to guess which facility became the victim of this closure—the Mound Correctional Facility. Remember, Alec and Wayman worked at Ryan, so the warden wasn't about to close that prison, where he was in absolute control. Even though Mound was the cleaner facility of the two, Mound was incorporated into Ryan. It was a no brainer to anyone who had been following the game, that this was just another step in the name of keeping the regime in power. But the problem that this regime would encounter was that they were playing a game of checkers instead of the game of chess.

Wayman and Alec were chomping at the bit to get at the staff at Mound, who they blamed for their transfer to Ryan instead of being accountable for their own behavior. Along the way, this gave the staff at Ryan a sense of relief knowing maybe they could get these two guys off their backs. A lot of the Ryan staff fell right in line with Alec and Wayman's ideas and were happy for it. Not all the staff there behaved in that manner, but about 75 percent of them did. Mound had more senior staff than Ryan did—experienced staff, with years of service, who weren't used to the regime. Yet, because the warden was in Alec and Wayman's pocket, a lot of experienced staff started to replace the lesser experienced staff out of Ryan Facility.

Whether it was supervisors, captains, lieutenants, sergeants, counselors, corrections officers, we, the Mound staff, were able to replace about 70 percent of the Ryan staff when the prisons were combined. But even though the Ryan staff was now predominantly experienced, straightforward, and rule-abiding, the regime was still in place due to their system of seniority at Ryan.

There was going to be a showdown as we began to move over laterally to Ryan Facility. The first transfer wave included about thirty Mound staff members, and the second wave included seventy; about one hundred staff members from Mound transferred next door, leaving about fifty original Ryan staff members remaining at the facility. This meant that the Mound staff outnumbered the Ryan staff, but instead of being a positive influence, this just meant that the Ryan staff was more defensive and aggressive toward their new coworkers. They felt they had to defend their territory to keep their regime in place.

The Mound Corrections Facility staff who weren't transferred to Ryan were relocated to Macomb Correctional Facility in the county of Macomb, Michigan. This was about a hundred corrections officers and five administrators, high upper-level staff, including corrections officers as well as deputy wardens who went to Macomb, so we were pretty much split-up between two facilities—Macomb Correctional Facility and Ryan Correctional Facility—with the majority of staff going into Ryan Correctional Facility.

Since Mound had more senior staff than Ryan, the Mound staff bumped out or removed a lot of Ryan Correctional Facility staff (officers, counselors, supervisors). This was another reason for Alec and Wayman to resent and mistreat the new staff: they were replacing many of the regime's loyal allies. Alec and Wayman had been escorted out of Mound Correctional Facility just two years before its closing and were now in charge at Ryan Correctional Facility.

Wayman was a powerful staff member who could have the state police dogs called in to the prison at any given time of day. He also had the power to assist in prosecuting staff, which meant that in terms of quid pro quo, he was the most powerful man in prison. Wayman would decide if a staff member would be charged criminally or not and would participate in the investigation. Everyone knew he was corrupt, so there was no question that he was willing to abuse these powers.

Wayman dressed professionally, in a suit with some slick shoes, preferably gator-skinned dress shoes. The shoes were slick and shiny, just like his personality. Even though Wayman was wearing a suit on the outside, what was underneath was questionable. Wayman was the type of man who might wear women's stockings under his clothing. Get the picture? Wayman preferred men to women—sexually speaking. Why any type of organization would allow this type of individual, a man who would wear women's stockings, to be in absolute control of a prison that was full of Alpha males is beyond me.

These prisoners were walking around naked and at the total mercy of the staff and administration. A man who might have even more incentive to abuse them shouldn't be given a position of power over such an already potentially hazardous population. Remember the rate of women staffers falling in love with prisoners and getting manipulated into all kinds of situations when prisoners found out about their attractions or loneliness. They could also do this with a man, especially if that man was already harassing them and giving them close proximity and access to his offices.

Wayman could and would come into the correctional facility at any given hour of the day or night, even though there was no administrative reason that he should be at work in the middle of the night. But because he was in such a powerful position, no one was in a position to challenge his behavior. Everyone just turned a blind eye, because they were too afraid of losing their job to expose their boss's corruption.

Wayman would have correctional staff call out prisoners and escort them to his office, where prisoners would be alone with him for hours at a time. I'm not kidding, this would actually occur. Again, there was no administrative reason that the inspector should be interviewing prisoners alone in the middle of the night for several hours. If this ever happened legitimately, it would be rare and not a regular occurrence.

What happened in Wayman's office? We can never know, because the only witnesses were the prisoners themselves. What we do know is that a powerful man who in many ways held these prisoners' lives in his hands, or at least the quality of their lives, was spending a lot of alone time with these vulnerable, strong, and attractive young men.

To my shock, Wayman would also do impromptu prison strip searches on the prisoners at the facility. During these strip searches, Wayman would want the prisoners to stand in a circle, about eight to ten prisoners at a time. Think of a round circle where eight to ten prisoners have to take off their clothing and be strip searched in front of Wayman, while he is looking on. In all my years of working in corrections, I have never seen the need for so many strip searches. Nor was there a need for the inspector to conduct these searches, which would be conducted by an officer. Wayman also conducted these searches quite differently from the way they were supposed to go.

Some of the prisoners would vigorously refuse, cursing and saying "I'm not down with this bullshit!" This would still be a minority of the prisoners, because anyone who objected would be locked up in solitary. Usually, of eight or ten prisoners, only two or three would object and have misconduct tickets written up and find themselves locked up. The remaining prisoners would agree to the search. They would agree to this humiliation because they did not need misconduct tickets in their files.

The misconduct tickets that we used to write-up prisoners wouldn't just affect their life inside the prison. Having a certain number of these tickets would affect prisoners' ability to get parole. Wayman wasn't just sexually harassing these prisoners; he was using their desire for freedom against them. If you wanted to get parole, you were supposed to do everything the corrections officers asked you to do. This was just as bad as police officers abusing their authority or threatening people with criminal charges if they didn't obey their orders. These prisoners had already been punished, and now their punishment could be extended not because they had done anything wrong but also because they weren't going along with the abuse of a person who was supposed to be helping them get back on the right track.

Many of these men would go along because they knew that if they did, they'd have a better chance of getting good write-ups instead of misconduct tickets. This meant seeing the outside world sooner rather than later, so it's no mystery why most of these prisoners went along. Wayman also provided the prisoners with stamps. Stamps were like coins in the prison, to trade for food, soap, and other basic necessities of life. Especially for those prisoners who did not have any money coming in from outside sources, to get stamps in exchange for sexual favors might have been the only way they could purchase these things. This could have been appealing to some, but it was still a terrible abuse of power on Wayman's part.

In this regime, the man who controlled the entire facility in which these prisoners lived—their food, shelter, and time—also had the power to keep them from their girlfriends, children, parents, and in short, their whole lives. Wayman was the chief of police at the Ryan Facility, which made him extremely powerful, because he could bring the dogs in on you. Nobody had a problem with anybody's sexual preferences, but this was like a fox in a henhouse or a kid in a candy store. Wayman had so much influence and power that the staff would never ever question any of his actions. He didn't just hold the prisoner's lives in the balance; he also held the jobs and lives of his staff in the balance. Anyone who went up against him risked losing an important foundation of their life—their job and their livelihood.

At one point, a few prisoners broke into Wayman's administration office. I'd like to know what's going on when prisoners want to and can break into the inspector's office. Who knows what else was in there. Personal information about officers and staff was found later in the rooms of prisoners. This meant that the prisoners had personal information about officers, including addresses and phone numbers. For some prisoners—the really connected lifers or gangsters—this information combined with a cell phone could mean a hit on a corrections officer's or administrator's family. At the very least, the fact that a prisoner might know where you live, or where any of your staff lives, could be used for serious blackmail inside the system to get prisoners access to contraband or even time away from prison, as in the case of the high-ranking gangster I mentioned earlier. The Department of Corrections certainly showed poor management in their hiring of some supervisors, but this goes back to that good old boy network of "If you scratch my back, I'll scratch yours."

Being a senior corrections officer at this time, I would notice all of these strange occurrences: high-ranking staff coming to work in the middle of the night, strip searches being conducted on prisoners, and prisoners being in possession of staff information. I also saw a lot of the unwanted behavior, and when I saw that Supervisor Wayman was present, I thought, "Something's wrong with this picture."

Supervisor Wayman's way of conducting strip searches was awkward and not how I had seen correctional staff conduct strip searches in the past. Wayman's methods violated the prisoners' rights. I thought, "What does he want—a sword fight?" What do I mean by a sword fight—having all these prisoners completely naked, standing around each other jousting? You get the picture?

It didn't take a rocket scientist to figure out that Wayman was interested in these strip searches for sexual gratification, not as an attempt to find and control contraband. Supervisor Wayman was in his glory, with no one to hold him accountable for any decisions he made or any actions he took, alone in his office with prisoners. He took that same demeanor that got him removed from Mound Correctional Facility over to Ryan. And he felt like the Mound staff was responsible for his removal from that facility, instead of admitting that he was responsible for his own position. When the prisons were combined, Wayman had to defend his position to keep having his cake and eating it too.

The other individual who was removed from Mound was named Alec. Alec could be described as a member of one of the famous movie families, the Baldwins, with that wild, stringy hair and those half-stoned looks on their faces. Supervisor Alec had more power than Wayman. Alec was technically Wayman's boss, but the two of them went hand in hand running the regime. They agreed on the way they would go about putting fear in the hearts and minds of staff members whom they didn't like—staff who wouldn't do what they wanted them to do. The staff learned this quickly and soon did what they wanted, more out of fear than loyalty.

Alec was more of a harasser, committing verbal harassment and even attempting sexual harassment against female staff and administration. His main weapon was quid pro quo or sexual harassment. The majority of the women who worked under his supervision and who wanted to be promoted had to go through Alec. That meant you were going to have to get up under his desk, way up under his desk, if you know what I mean. Female staff and officers were subjected to the humiliation that comes with the man who holds your job, maybe your kids' meals, in his hands to exploit you for sex.

That was part of his DNA. I don't know where that demeanor came from, but once Alec was in that position, any woman who wanted a position under his watch had to come through him. The old boys' club was particularly important here because these women didn't feel that they had anyone to go to in order to report these crimes. If they admitted that they had been the victim of Alec's sexual harassment, they ran the risk of another administrator trying to do the same thing.

For example, there was a time a female prison guard fell in love with a prisoner, and she would talk on the office phone to the prisoner, who apparently was on a phone in another housing unit. A chaplain notified the authorities of this incident. Alec used this to his advantage, making sure that she—the corrections officer—would have to do whatever he wanted after he found out about this incident. Once he had this information to use against her, he moved her into a high-ranking position. This meant that he could control her, because if she ever wanted to expose him, he would expose her. Essentially he also controlled any staff she supervised, because if any important decisions came to her, she had to listen to him.

These types of situations are what would get Alec in trouble with other staff members, and eventually one of the correctional staff, a woman he had treated this way, filed sexual-harassment charges against him. The State did not want this abuser to be exposed, so they settled the matter with her. The administration didn't want bad press, so they essentially paid this woman to stay quiet. What they did not do was remove Alec from power. This meant that he was free to continue his behavior, getting a steady paycheck the whole time.

The staff at Ryan was in a permanent state of fear and dysfunction. They had no choice in any decision making. The entire staff was basically a staff of puppets for these two individuals and the warden at the time, who allowed the two supervisors to run rampant about the facility—reckless and abusive. This type of unprofessional behavior is unacceptable anywhere and would be prevented elsewhere throughout the Department of Corrections, yet it was prevalent at this facility. It makes you wonder why a warden would allow this to go on, creating a hostile work environment and pitting staff against one another.

Maybe there was something going on that they didn't want the subordinates or lower-level staff to know about. The warden had to have been very mean spirited to be so willing to find his staff guilty of any little infraction. It was said that "any disciplinary packets that came to his desk were immediately heard, and you were found to be guilty, before even presenting your defense against any allegations." This was brought to the staff's attention at Mound, so we knew that we were about to transfer into this hostile environment.

So when I say that Ryan Correctional Facility seemed as though it was being run by a regime, like the Communist Regime, the Taliban Regime, or ISIL, these abuses are what I'm talking about. Transferring to Ryan, the Mound staff knew they were about to witness all this firsthand. Alec and Wayman were just chomping at the bit to get at the corrections officers at Mound, whom they blamed for their downfall and who were now coming into the facility that they controlled. They were now two of the three top supervisors over the staff that was coming into their facility. This would bring about tension and hostility among the correctional staff of both facilities. Ryan's correctional staff were told by the two supervisors that the incoming staff "were lazy, had no work ethic, and were not to be trusted."

The staff at Ryan didn't know the staff at Mound, so they believed what they heard and bought into these accusations. Not all but the majority of the staff believed what they had been told because they were looking for any relief from the oppression that they were encountering daily. Why not? When you're working under such an oppressive environment, it's easy for relief to be your only goal, especially if you don't believe improvement is possible. They thought this would help position those staff members who were left at that facility into cushy positions and favorable friendships with the supervisory regime and it did.

On the other hand, the correctional staff coming from next door, over the hill, at Mound, knew that we had to stick together as a team. This was not a staff of just one nationality; we had a mixed group of black, white, and Hispanic staff, who got along quite well and were experienced at working together.

Remember, we had done a lot of community events, sports, and picnics outside of work, so we were extremely familiar with each other and trusted each other, even outside of the work context. We knew the importance of dividing and conquering, like Alec and Wayman were doing. We knew that this led to low morale. At one point in time, about two weeks before we were to report to the Ryan Correctional Facility, one of my white counterparts—a corrections officer—approached me.

"You know, we will all have to stick together," he said, "because of those two individuals, Alec and Wayman. You know how they view and feel about the incoming staff."

"Yeah, I know," I said.

"They're out to get us," he said, and I agreed.

But we just left it at that.

It was unbelievable that any governmental staff would have to go through these hostile conditions from any supervisory staff, but we were about to. I myself didn't really endure any harassment or hostilities personally when the first wave of corrections officers arrived at the facility. I was one of the top corrections officers with twenty-seven years of experience in the Department of Corrections, so Alec and Wayman weren't going to mess with me. I had an impeccable record and a reputation for honesty and straightforwardness. One thing those individuals did respect was the fact that there were some senior officers who had been at other top, well-respected correctional facilities and that I was one of those individuals.

There were thirteen others, in addition to myself, who were not targeted. But knowing that our coworkers—who were inside a correctional facility, working to keep the state of Michigan citizens safe from convicted criminals and criminal activities that stretch into the communities—were enduring this treatment didn't sit well with the fourteen staff members who had first arrived at Ryan Correctional Facility.

So the staff who came from Mound would get together and talk about ways to bring this to the attention of higher administrative staff outside of the facility. You may think, what kind of correctional work was going on if all of this mess was happening? This is a good question. Again, we were professional staff doing the correctional work of maintaining safety and security. These goals were always first and foremost in our minds. We completed our job assignments completely before trying to address the problems in the administration.

It appeared to me that this regime was playing a game of checkers when they thought they were playing chess with the staff from Mound. They assumed that we were powerless checker pieces that they could move at will, when in fact we all had our own particular strengths to draw on in order to get the job done and stand up against what corruption we could.

Like a team of chess pieces, the staff from Mound could unite toward a common goal and accomplish more together than we could apart. The lieutenants and supervisors would be the knights, who could move around corners and over other pieces. The sergeants or supervisors would be the rooks, who could move many squares at a time and protect other pieces with their stalwartness. The remaining correctional officers would be the pawns, who might only be able to move one square at a time—but remember, if a pawn stays alive long enough and gets to the other end of the board, it can be swapped for a lost piece. So a pawn can become a rook or a bishop or even a queen. If a pawn sticks at it long enough, it can become one of the most powerful pieces on the board.

It was bad enough pitting the staff at Ryan and Mound against each other, which appeared to be a game of checkers, bouncing us all around the facility. The Mound staff were not interested in playing games. They were there to do the job that they applied for, and they understood how to run a correctional facility. Now that the first wave of corrections officers had arrived, it didn't take long for Alec and Wayman to show who had control of the facility. They wanted to demonstrate their power so that none of the Mound staff would have the courage to step out of their place.

There was an incident, a simple incident that happened, showing what kind of environment the Mound staff had to deal with. Frank, a Senior Mound Correctional Officer, was harshly chastised by one of the lieutenant-knights about being late for work. Now, Frank was very experienced and was part of the union staff at Mound; he was set to retire in about eight months.

Within his first week of transferring to Ryan, Frank was running a little late to work but only by four or five minutes. Now, this was this lieutenant-knight's first and only contact with this newly arrived staff member, and their initial conversation went like this:

"You're late," said the lieutenant-knight. "I'm going to let the warden know about this."

Frank wasn't the kind of guy to take any nonsense from anyone, and he was only eight months from retirement. He wasn't about to let this young guy treat him this way.

"How dare you threaten me with talk of letting the warden know about me being late four or five minutes," Frank said. "You and the warden can go to hell!"

This shocked the lieutenant-knight, but in such an environment of fear, he backed down from Frank.

I just happened to be behind Frank as he was speaking, and the lieutenant-knight's behavior angered me as well. I was surprised this came out of his mouth. That was not necessary, especially during a staff transition. The lieutenant-knight should have tried to embrace this connection with the new staff member, but apparently he was told to report anything and everything to the warden-king.

Why should any simple situation such as being four or five minutes late for work be sent this far up the chain of command to the warden? As the other group of corrections officers arrived—the other fifty or sixty—the hostility got more and more palpable. Remember, the staff at Ryan was told the Mound staff was horrible, lazy, and disengaged. The two individual administrators who were removed from Mound were about to show the staff at Ryan their dominance by bullying and displaying their willingness to harass and abuse.

They humiliated the second round of staff by having them remove their shoes and empty their pockets before they were allowed through the secured entrance of the prison—the entrance the staff used to enter and exit the prison. This was not procedure and was, again, entirely unnecessary to the tasks at hand of maintaining safety and order in the prison. This staff strip search was a strut of power by the Ryan staff.

What would make any administrative staff do this to their incoming staff is beyond me. But this did happen. The fourteen of us who had arrived before this group were now on the day shift and were not subjected to this mess. We heard about what had happened—the staff strip search—from our coworkers. This news made us incredibly angry. Many of us were already familiar with Alec and Wayman and knew that this was just them playing their same old games. And we were pissed off.

It was almost impossible to disguise our anger around the Ryan staff. The hostility was apparent now more than ever, and the correctional officers—the pawns from Ryan—were liking what they saw going on with the staff from Mound. They weren't the only ones being oppressed anymore, and that felt good to them.

There were other incidents during this time, where Alec and Wayman, the two top supervisors under the warden-king, had been involved in incidents that validated the fact that this was a bully regime. Wayman, as you may recall, was the supervisor who liked to wear nylon stockings under his pants, and Alec would look for bullying and sexual-harassment opportunities with any female staff or officer.

At one point, Alec and Wayman backed a very good and professional staff member into a corner and even physically pushed him into Alec's office.

Wayman had demanded that the staff member come to the area, and when the staff member arrived, they started double-teaming him to manifest their power.

Wayman said, "I heard you were talking about my boss down in your work area. I don't appreciate you talking about my boss."

Alec, the boss in question, was standing there, staring and listening to this garbage by his coadministrator. Of course, the staff member was probably scared and denied saying anything, especially since Alec was right there in the room.

Then Alec said, "I should slap the shit out of you. Get the fuck out of my area; I should fire you."

This was talk you might expect from a prisoner but not from a high-ranking administrator at the height of his power. There was no reason to speak this way to a staff member who had the right to say what he wanted about his boss during his downtime.

When I heard about this incident, Alec and Wayman's actions were very disturbing to me. The other staff who had heard about this were also upset and disturbed. Alec was not even a correctional officer, just an administrative staff member. After we heard about this incident and knew about the other incidents that had occurred, someone had to step up and nip this in the bud, so to speak.

I then took this as a challenge, maybe a chess challenge, so to speak.

I was dealing with a regime that had the backing of the State of Michigan Department of Corrections. Remember, the warden and other administration had gotten away with simply moving Alec and Wayman when they had both been caught abusing their power at Mound. They didn't feel like they could be touched, disciplined, or confronted by any of their subordinates.

These two men, because they controlled our workplace, felt they had all the staff jobs and livelihoods under their control. Anyone just starting out, especially, had no ability to challenge them, because it was your word against theirs. As an experienced staff member, I could see the divisiveness, the anger, and the harassment that was going on at this facility, perpetrated by those two individuals, Wayman (the queen) and Alec (the bishop), and cosigned by the warden-king.

At this point, I started to step up and calm the staff at Ryan who had come from Mound and assured them that things would change. I tried to tell them that it wasn't hopeless and that we wouldn't have to endure this treatment forever. Thankfully, things did start to change, and quickly.

All of this was happening within two months of the closing of Mound Prison Facility. There was so much corruption and abuse during the closing and combining of the prisons that it tended to make me believe that a lot of these incidents were premeditated, and the incidents as well as the cover-ups were conspired. It's unusual enough to have this level of corruption in a prison, in my experience, but it's even stranger that it all functioned so broadly and so smoothly. I'm sure that there were even more instances of corruption at Ryan before the Mound staff started arriving there to witness it.

The above incidents happened in November and December 2011. By January 2012 and up until January 2014, things would take a turn for the worse for the regime who appeared to be playing a game of checkers instead of chess. In a chess game, you have to have patience. Chess is a thinking person's game. Life itself is a thinking person's game, with ups and downs that everyone must weather. During approaching storms, one must stay afloat, own up to his or her responsibilities, and be accountable for his or her own actions.

Alec and Wayman had the support of the supervisors under them, who did the dirty work and got the pleasure of not being bothered by Alec and Wayman and the chance to move up the ladder and to get better-paid positions. People were getting promoted because they would do whatever Alec and Wayman told them to do instead of the job they should do. They were controlling the staff and not the prisoners, because the people in charge had hidden agendas.

Within two years, the regime would go through a wave of pressure and investigation. The pressure cooker would eventually erupt and lead to one of the most important pieces on the chess board—the warden-king—getting escorted out of the correctional facility by three individuals in white shirts and ties, driving black Escalades.

It took a combination of events, including the murder of an abusive supervisor elsewhere in the Michigan Corrections System, for the statewide administration to finally address what was happening at the now-combined facility.

Their downfall started when the staff from Mound who had come over to Ryan got together and wrote a letter to the director of the Department Heads of State (EEOC, Internal Affairs, and Director's Office). By writing to all of these administrators at once, the author of the letter ensured that it would be taken seriously. The administrators could not ignore a letter that was addressed to four other people, because if they tried to cover up the accusations instead of investigating them, they ran the risk that another administrator would expose their corruption.

The letter was written by a person named Timothy Sutton, though there is no record of any Timothy Sutton working for the Michigan Department of Corrections.

## Chapter 4

# WHO IS TIMOTHY SUTTON?

The game-changing letter from Timothy Sutton couldn't have arrived at a more stressful or complicated time for the Michigan Department of Corrections. In late 2010, a risky harassment situation ended in a tragedy that began a dramatic shift in the department's tolerance for abusive staff members.

After finishing his shift one evening at one of Michigan's state prisons, a guard named Rodney Hays clocked out of work, as he had every other day for ten years. Instead of leaving right away, he lingered in the parking lot of the prison until his supervisor had also clocked out and gotten into his car. Hays followed the supervisor to the gas station located nearby, where so many staff members went after a long day working in the prison to get a soda or a bag of chips for the drive home or a lottery ticket that promised at least a few seconds of the possibility of retiring early on a beach somewhere. But Rodney Hays wasn't buying a snack or a lottery ticket or a frozen dinner to eat alone in front of his TV. He parked alongside the supervisor in the gas station parking lot, drew his gun, and shot the supervisor, killing him almost immediately.

I immediately paid close attention to this story because I had witnessed so much abuse and harassment among the staff that I had long wondered what was the worst that could happen. One guard killing another was certainly the worst that I could have imagined. While we'll never know exactly what happened, there were rumors that the supervisor was verbally abusive to Hays, harassing him at work and even calling him at home to continue the harassment.

Hays was a mild-mannered officer who hadn't been involved in any violent incidents or dramas throughout his career. Nothing about him indicated that he was capable of murder. The supervisor was newer, part of the new generation of officers and administrators who came in as a result of the War on Drugs and the inflated populations in the prisons. The new supervisor was trained to be hard-nosed, to be harsh, and to control the officers under his command as severely as he saw fit. The supervisor looked at Hays as being weak, because Hays was an older guard who had spent his career in the less militaristic climate of the seventies and eighties.

The young supervisor was undoubtedly on a power trip, being hard and unfair toward Hays. I also suspect that Hays's many years in corrections could have slowly worn away at his ability to tolerate this type of behavior from anyone. In any case, an otherwise peaceful man snapped and killed his supervisor. Hays tried to commit suicide but lived. He's now serving out his sentence inside a prison just like the one he was about to retire from.

There was no way to keep the murder of a guard (especially a murder outside the prison walls) a secret from the public. This story soon traveled through the department, and also throughout the public, bringing a new level of public scrutiny upon the Michigan Department of Corrections. There was no hiding this story or sweeping it under the rug and hoping that no one noticed it.

The story immediately reminded me of the abuses I had witnessed and heard about happening at the hands of Alec and Wayman. I could only imagine how many guards, young and old, had come close to cracking under the regime that these two and their warden-king had created. During the fury of national and local press attention that followed the murder of the supervisor, I became more and more convinced that someone had to take action against the dangerous regime before anyone got more seriously hurt. The shooting of one officer by another had brought some very negative attention on the department, calling into question the integrity of the whole corrections system. The system was supposed to be a place where bad men became good men, but it had revealed itself to also be a place where good men became bad men.

In 2011 the atmosphere was still tense within the Michigan Department of Corrections. That year, a letter from someone named Timothy Sutton arrived at the offices of five different department heads within the Michigan Correctional Department. As the Mound Facility prepared to close, a letter arrived for the director of the Department of Corrections and several other department heads, five administrators in all. Since Sutton sent the letter to five different departments, they had to act on it, because they got it at the same time:

> Dear Director of Corrections, EEOC, Communications, Etc.,
>
> Someone from your office should come down to the Ryan Correctional Facility and deal with the hostile work environment here, which includes sexual and verbal harassment of both prisoners and female staff, as well as intimidation and coercion of all staff. The staff has endured this environment since the integration of Mound and Ryan prison staff in November 2011. We know how you feel about the values and the vision of the Department of Corrections, and that you talk about holding these leaders accountable for their actions. Someone can possibly get seriously hurt if an intervention does not take place. I don't think that this would be a good time for something like this to occur, considering the damaging public relations from the Hays incident at Wayne Correctional Facility last year.
>
> Sincerely,
> Timothy Sutton

The Michigan Department of Corrections was in no position to fight another scandal in the press. When they received this letter from Mr. Sutton, they sent someone down from Lansing to Mound-Ryan, to deal with the matter immediately. Besides all of the department heads who received these letters from Timothy Sutton, Internal Affairs had to anticipate and immediately deflate any notions that this letter landed on their desk and they did nothing about it. The administrators had to make it known that they had responded right away to these abuses, which had been occurring under their supposedly watchful eyes. They wanted it to be known that these things would not be allowed to happen on their watch. Lansing sent an Internal Affairs Division member to Ryan Correctional Facility to get to the bottom of the accusations set forth in the letter.

After very little investigation, almost immediately, Internal Affairs announced that Alec would be transferred to another prison, five hours away from Ryan. Rather than pursuing any official charges against him or removing him from having the opportunity to abuse again, the department's first idea was to move him and hope that the problem would go away. Internal Affairs had the power to appoint people to positions across the Michigan Corrections System, to lose problematic people in the system rather than taking responsibility for what they had done. Even at this moment of exposure, Alec seemed to have power. Alec refused to be transferred, and instead of facing charges, demotion, or unemployment, Alec was given the option to retire.

When a person gets that high up in an institution, they're at the appointment of the directors, who at that point have been getting information on them for years. They didn't need to investigate Alec; Alec's files were muddy, and this was just the straw that broke the camel's back, as far as they were concerned. The administration didn't seem worried about what would happen if Alec was given another job in the same position of being able to abuse prisoners or staff. They wanted to avoid scandal but not enough to actually charge their staff member with the crimes they knew he had committed. They were more concerned with figuring out the identity of the snitch, Timothy Sutton.

In addition to the investigator who was looking into Alec and Wayman, Internal Affairs also sent someone down to the facility to talk to nearly twenty members of the Mound Correctional staff who had come over to Ryan Correctional Facility. It was assumed that Timothy Sutton was a Mound staff member, but again, if the administration was just learning about all these abuses, they would have no way of knowing that.

The Internal Affairs investigators would start every interview with the same question, grilling each member of the Mound staff like we were all part of a crime show episode.

They'd shine the light in our eyes, so to speak, and they'd ask, "Are you Timothy Sutton?"

They got the same answer from every staff member who had come from Mound. "No," everyone said, one after the other.

"Do you know who Timothy Sutton is?" they'd ask, sure that someone knew and was covering up the identity of the letter writer.

"No," they would hear, again and again.

They asked the same questions to the Ryan staff, but they received the same answers from them. No one claimed any knowledge of or connection with Sutton. The Lansing Department of Corrections really wanted to know who Timothy Sutton was, but none of the fifteen or twenty corrections officers from Mound knew who Timothy Sutton was, and the officers from Ryan certainly couldn't imagine anyone who had the guts to stand up to their boss, who had kept them terrorized for most of their careers.

Even as the investigators were interviewing the ex-Mound Correctional officers, Alec and Wayman, the supervisors at the heart of all of this hostility were still abusing their powers. Alec used the last weeks before his retirement to continue and defend his regime, even though it meant exposing himself to more charges even while the investigators were there. But Alec was obviously unconcerned about the possibility of consequences for his actions. To him there was nothing to worry about.

I was especially aware that Alec and Wayman were verbally and physically harassing a noncustody staff member, Leon, who had recently come over from next door. They had the audacity to corner this noncustody staff member and bump him, which is considered physical intimidation according to the rules of conduct at the prison.

Apparently, Alec had gotten some intelligence on Leon—that Leon was saying something about him or Wayman. Alec was focused on telling Leon to keep quiet.

Alec cornered Leon, trying to intimidate him physically, and said, "If I hear you say my name from any of my staff, I'm going to fire your ass."

Wayman, who was standing nearby, said, "I should slap the shit out of you!" to Leon.

Of course, Leon was intimidated and had no desire from then on to discuss the conditions of the prison with anyone unless he absolutely had to.

Now, neither one of these two individuals were gangsters; they just had the power of being State of Michigan administrators. To me, both supervisors were something out of *The Wizard of Oz*, as the Lion (with no courage) and the Scarecrow (with no brain), along with their fearless leader, the warden, who was the Tin Man (with no heart).

Alec and Wayman's acts of intimidation were brought to the attention of the Internal Affairs investigators, while they were still at the facility. This was late January or early February 2012. By April 2012, Alec was relieved of his duties as a supervisor at Ryan Correctional Facility. It was believed that he was being sent to a correctional facility three hours the opposite way from where he lived, but he was not going to accept that fate.

Remember, when you are an appointed official in this capacity, you are under the director's authority and power, which can place you wherever the director deems necessary; you could be placed in the Upper Peninsula, far from where anyone wanted to be. Alec instead chose to exit stage right and retire. Alec was a fighter but didn't have anybody left to fight or anyone to sue. Who was he gonna sue? Timothy Sutton?

Alec's counterpart, Wayman, was bumped from Ryan to a prison far away. Since he had less seniority than another supervisor at the Ryan-Mound Facility, he was transferred to another facility in Macomb County. That had to be a very powerful letter that was sent the department heads. Alec and Wayman even had some of their people saying that they had written the letter, in an attempt to pressure the letter writer into revealing himself.

You might be wondering who Timothy Sutton was. He could have been any of the employees who worked at Ryan or Mound; the important thing was that he was the person who drafted a letter to those department heads within the State of Michigan in order to confront the abuses that were rampant at our facility. Someone from the Internal Affairs Division needed to come conduct an investigation of the blatant harassment and hostilities that were going on at this facility, and Timothy Sutton set that very thing into motion with his letter.

But now the regime was crumbling. Two of the three most powerful chess pieces had been removed, but the warden still had the rooks, his lieutenants, the knights, his sergeants, and the pawns, the Ryan corrections officers on his team. Some of these corrections officers were stunned, left in shock and awe, unable to believe what had just happened before their eyes. Their fearless leaders, Alec and Wayman, were gone. It was a lot like a documentary I saw about the Civil War: when the slaves were emancipated, they didn't know where to go or what to do with their freedom. These pawns, the corrections officers, were sure their fearless leaders would return and made statements expressing this belief.

"They will be back," they'd say, and others would say hopefully, "They're just gone for a minute..."

This was sad to hear coming from officers from that facility, but they really believed that their beloved leaders, Wayman and Alec, would return. This would never happen, because the Department of Corrections didn't need any more problems in the press at that time. They didn't like that two of their top supervisors were removed from a facility, because to them that indicated that the staff had been given too much power. That's not how correctional facilities are supposed to work. There's supposed to be a balance of power, not a concentration of it at the top. Now the air in the regime had deflated; two of the king's pieces had fallen; the warden-king, his queen (Wayman), and his bishop (Alec) were displaced and shaken in their power. But now that Alec and Wayman were gone, any problems would be attributed to the most powerful person left, the warden-king.

Now, the staff at Ryan could go about their jobs of fighting crime from the inside of the correctional facility and maintaining some order among the prisoners. Six months into 2012, the year that the two pieces fell, a new supervisor took the position vacated by Alec. The new supervisor would prove to be very professional and competent, knowing the ins and outs of how to perform his job. This was the summer of 2012, and Ryan's staff, who were released from the control and supervision of the regime, were finally finding out what it was like to experience togetherness as a staff and the enormity of what coming together for a cause could bring about.

During the summer and into the fall, the correction staff were coming together. We were being thanked instead of hassled for our strong will and determination, for standing up against those hostile individuals. The Ryan staff were still in shock, however; but that was okay with us—the Mound staff—since their shock was positive—they were shocked at actually coming to a relatively safe place each day and being able to do their work.

The events that happened in September 2012, would further shake the staff at Ryan Correctional Facility. This is where I come in; I was completely involved with everything that was going on from this point until January 2014. Remember, all of this would occur within a two-year span from December 2011 to December 2013 and January 2014.

During this time, I was asked to do shakedowns of prisoners, their cells, and prisoners in certain areas by the new administrator who, by the way, came from Mound Corrections Facility and had himself been degraded by those two corrupt chess pieces—the queen and the bishop of the regime. The new administrator had a position of the same status as Alec (a bishop), but he was not given any power by the warden-king because of his affiliation with the Mound staff. But when those two individuals were removed, he was left with the sole authority to run the institution, while still under the warden's power.

The new administrator had his own sergeants and lieutenants, whom he trusted to go about the real business of corrections (maintaining order, having a contraband-free facility, and creating camaraderie among staff), which is what we had at Mound Correctional Facility.

The new administrator called on me to help him establish some order and simultaneously earn the respect of the lieutenants, captains, and sergeants from Mound Correctional Facility. He knew that I had a reputation for being responsible, respectful, and aboveboard. I had no problem stepping up to the challenge and helping them clean up whatever they needed me to do. I was being called on a lot between June and September of 2013. At times I was taken away from my regular assignments to shakedown individual cells of prisoners, and what I was finding was becoming disturbing to me.

Remember, although Alec and Wayman were removed, their abuses weren't over. They had allowed a whole system of corruption to take over the prison, which meant that contraband was being smuggled, traded, and sold and that many staff members were in on the illegal activity, from staff inside the prison walls to drivers or deliverymen who had occasional access to the prison, in addition to outside individuals who visited prisoners to pass contraband under the willing eyes of corrupt guards. Alec and Wayman had supervised all of this in exchange for being able to commit their own abuses of a more personal, sexual nature. Just because they had left the building, it didn't mean that all of these other systems were going to disappear. They were already in place, but now there were more watchful eyes on them. Now that an honest supervisor was in charge, and I was in charge of searching so many prisoners, contraband was actually being discovered and reported instead of being ignored and allowed to pass through the prison.

In all my years of working as a prison guard, I had never seen such quantities of contraband. Michigan State Prisons were nonsmoking facilities, period, because it made no sense to allow prisoners to smoke and then pay for their increased health care when they had health problems due to smoking. This was a hard-line policy in Michigan Corrections. Yet I found large quantities of tobacco and cigarette products in the rooms of prisoners. I also found cell phones on individual prisoners—prisoners who were doing life or fifteen to twenty-five years in prison. This was especially dangerous because these long-term prisoners could use the phones to control their assets on the outside.

Remember, this was a prison, not a retirement home. These men who were serving life were incredibly dangerous. If they had a cell phone, it meant that they could virtually run a criminal empire from prison, which meant that they were being inconvenienced but not stopped by the justice system. With a cell phone, an inmate is able to manipulate their appeals cases, run drugs or other contraband through the prison system, control criminal networks on the outside, and even order hits on their enemies, which could easily include guards and their families.

Now, I was wondering what was going on; it shouldn't be so easy to find such serious contraband. We were getting into something big, but I had no idea what. I was one of the senior staff members, but I had never seen anything like this. This administrator trusted me because of our time together at the Mound Facility next door. I wouldn't let him down.

I did often think, "Come on, get a younger staff member to do this work, I'm two years away from being able to retire!"

I said this to myself but not to anyone else. The most important things to me were professionalism and being a team player. That, and knowing what the staff had already had to put up with, kept me from turning down the difficult assignment of cleaning up Alec and Wayman's messes. I could not say no.

The identity of Timothy Sutton remained a mystery; when the original investigators had arrived to investigate Sutton's accusations, everyone was quick to deny that they were Timothy Sutton or that they knew anything about him. But after Alec was removed and things started to get cleaned up, it wasn't uncommon to hear someone bragging in the hallway that he was Timothy Sutton and that he had gotten all of this positive change going.

I wasn't about to tell anyone the truth about who Timothy Sutton was. I was content to know that he had made a powerful contribution beyond what anyone could have anticipated. Instead of moving one space at a time, like a pawn in the service of the king, Timothy Sutton had overturned the whole board. He wasn't a pawn; he was a player.

## Chapter 5

# GAME CHANGER/THE COVER-UP

As the end of August came to a close, the correctional facility workers and prisoners were going through their daily routines, which included various activities, school programs, recreational activities, and cleaning up the facility grounds. The regime seemed to have utterly collapsed, and the warden-king had started to take a different approach toward the newer correctional staff. These new staff members had arrived from the closed facility and hadn't been exposed to the regime at its height. The warden-king changed his attitude toward the staff dramatically during this time. At one point, he even suggested to a couple of the correctional staff members that there was the possibility of having a staff potluck dinner—a type of community outing at the facility. To me, this meant that either he was trying to bring the staff together or he was trying to make himself look more favorable toward the staff. Given his track record, I assume it would be the latter, since the warden-king was always more interested in controlling the staff community than he was in community building.

Remember, the warden-king did not have his inspector, Wayman (the queen), or his deputy warden, Alec (the bishop), around to influence him. I was open to the possibility that maybe he was correcting his own behavior now that he was outside of their influence. They were both long gone by this time. So what else could he do but try to get along with the staff that was left there with him? What I didn't realize was that the warden-king still had quite a few chess pieces left in his arsenal, even if the most powerful pieces had been taken off the board. The warden-king still had his lieutenants (knights), a few sergeants (rooks), and a supporting cast of correctional officers (pawns), who were still working under him at the correctional facility. So there was still a decent level of comfort for the warden-king to carry on whatever agenda he had or to continue whatever illegal activities had been going on under the supervision of Alec (bishop) and Wayman (queen).

But in the middle of 2012, a new inspector arrived to replace Wayman. This inspector also came from the closed correction facility, and he turned out to be a true professional. This meant that he performed his job correctly, for the safety and security of the prison, and didn't let bribes or power influence him to let certain things go that might benefit the warden-king. Soon, the new inspector would get some information about a troubling scenario at the correctional facility, which a group of prisoners (not staff) wanted to expose. The fact that prisoners wanted to expose this activity is significant because this means that the situation was bad enough—the corruption was so thorough—that prisoners were more worried about it than staff members were.

The inspector received a letter or kite, which is a letter written on prison stationary. The letter came from a prisoner—a state informant. I myself didn't know this prisoner or the situation, nor did any other staff whom I knew. This letter would start the final collapse of the regime and initiate the downfall of the warden-king once and for all.

On September 24, 2012, three correction staff members were called to the new inspector's office to read a letter or kite that was written by a state informant and prisoner. The letter exposed a contraband enterprise and mentioned three specific rooms where staff should search for contraband. Whoever wrote this letter also spoke about a group of prisoners who wanted to "kill a correctional officer at the Ryan Correctional State Facility."

The informant prisoner claimed that he had overheard this group of prisoners discussing their plan to murder a corrections officer. The informant prisoner then exchanged words with this group of prisoners.

The informant claimed to have approached the group, saying, "Come on, you guys need to rethink this; you can't kill a corrections officer."

Someone in the group had just replied, "Fuck that shit; we don't care about those officers."

The informant went on to say, "They had homemade cuff keys, drugs, and cell phones." He wrote that if the readers of his letter didn't believe him, they could call up north to a correctional facility in the UP and ask them. The informant had written vaguely that he had "helped them with a criminal investigation."

All of this was written in a letter to the new inspector. The new inspector shared the letter with three corrections officers. He told us that he wanted the three of us to read the letter, and then he dispatched us to three different rooms within one particular housing unit at the correctional facility.

The letter itself was very disturbing, and the inspector knew that he was about to uncover a complicated web of corruption; hence, he didn't trust just any staff to take on this task. The inspector felt that any other officer would probably be in on the corruption and smuggling, and on discovering the contraband, he would just hide the evidence and pretend that he hadn't found anything. When the inspector chose me as one of the officers he trusted to perform this task, I felt validated in my reputation for being an honest, straightforward officer who wasn't susceptible to corruption.

I had been called on other assignments just before this incident by my immediate supervisors, along with a few others, and we were putting a severe dent in the amount of contraband that was flowing through the correctional facility. This time, we expected to uncover a fair amount of contraband that had been allowed to exist during the height of the regime, but we had no idea what we were in for on this particular day.

I, for one, was at the tail end of my career in corrections, and I was really trying to maintain my professional work ethics and do anything that needed to be done to clean up the mess left behind by Alec (bishop) and Wayman (queen). I was definitely hoping that the less experienced staff would get the opportunity to learn and grow through these types of assignments and that I would be able to supervise the learning and growing, rather than putting in all the elbow work myself! But I guess the inspector didn't think this was an assignment for inexperienced correctional officers, and when I made the discovery, I understood why. Nothing in my long career had prepared me for the breadth of corruption we were about to discover, and most younger, more inexperienced officers would have lacked the maturity or job security that was necessary to deal with such a high-pressure situation.

So after being summoned to the inspector's office, we three—the three correctional officers the new inspector had chosen to put his faith in—we weren't going to let him down. Not now, especially after reading the letter that stated they wanted to kill an officer. With the chaos of all the recent transition and the staff and prisoners undergoing so much change, it was possible to imagine such a thing taking place. It was part of our job to imagine it and prevent it, but seeing the words in black and white, that it was possibly being planned right under our noses, made it a real possibility rather than just one of the many things that could go wrong inside a prison.

We were told to look for a homemade cuff key and other contraband that was mentioned in the letter. The room I was assigned to contained what I still call the mother lode of contraband. As I approached the room, I could see the prisoner sitting at his desk, rolling up some substance. On seeing me, he made one swift motion and swept everything he had on his table into the toilet and then flushed. Of course, this immediately told me that I was looking in the right direction and put the prisoner on guard.

I opened his cell and asked him to come out.

"C'mon, man," he said.

"Get out here," I demanded.

"I wasn't doing anything," he said, trying to distract me.

"I'm giving you an order, prisoner," I said in the most professional way that I could under the circumstances. "You need to exit this cell immediately."

"What for?" he asked, and I knew that he was stalling, because disobeying an order from an officer could mean time in solitary, but this prisoner was willing to risk that in order to distract me from my purpose and possibly persuade me not to make him leave his room.

"Now," I said, "or you'll be in trouble for insubordination, in addition to whatever I find in here."

Reluctantly, the prisoner straightened up with his last bit of pride and walked as nonchalantly as he could into the hallway, where the two other corrections officers stood. Within a few minutes, the prisoner was escorted to a holding area, and it was safe to search his room.

The first thing I saw was a blackberry cell phone plugged in and charging on the inmate's bed, as if it were any other bed in a normal home in America. But it wasn't; cell phones in prison are extremely dangerous. After finding the cell phone, I saw a taped-up cardboard box on the prisoner's bed. This sort of box should have contained family photos or, at worst, a stash of snacks or a few cigarettes. But what I found was the makings of dozens of cigarettes, which meant that this was a headquarters inside the prison black market. The box contained compressed tobacco, at least ten packs of rolling papers, and some crazy glue. I placed these items, as well as the cell phone and cord, on the counselor's desk.

Searching the rest of the room, I discovered the homemade cuff key that was mentioned in the kite, as well as a scalpel, which was very sharp and could have easily been used as a weapon. I gave all of these items to my supervisors, who turned them over to the new inspector for evidence. On top of the prisoner's locker, I found ten or eleven bars of hollowed-out soap bars within a plastic bag. At first I didn't understand why these would be hidden or why anyone would have such a collection of soap, but I knew something must be up because it was so unusual to have carved out, hollow soap bars in a cell.

I continued to shakedown the room methodically, taking my time, but I did not find anything else in the prisoner's property other than these ten or eleven bars of white soap inside of a footlocker that, upon further inspection, appeared to still be sealed in plastic as if they were new.

As I held one of these new-looking, fat bars of white soap in my hand, I noticed a bubbly type of fume on the clear plastic, and the bar of soap itself felt softer than usual. I tore open the plastic and bent the bar of soap in half, which was easy because it was so soft. The bar of otherwise harmless soap cracked apart to reveal a brand new cell phone—a flip phone—wrapped tightly in plastic. I continued to open the other bars of soap and found more contraband in them. Soap bars are not threatening in the hands of convicted criminals; it's usually a form of currency within a prison system, a barter system to each other, a bar of soap could be the most important item for paying off a debt.

After opening four other bars of soap, I found four more flip phones, and there were still six bars of soap left. I didn't make any assumptions and opened these as well. This thorough investigation turned out to mean the discovery of even more essential evidence. Two bars of soap appeared to contain marijuana, compressed and tightly packaged in plastic, and two other bars contained small packages wrapped tightly in gray duct tape, which probably meant more valuable, more highly restricted drugs such as cocaine. The last two soap bars were found inside purple-colored rubber-glove fingers, which may have contained heroine.

At this time, I stepped back and took a break, knowing that this was something way too big and out of the ordinary. Most contraband that comes into a correctional facility throughout this country is spread out very quickly, very thoroughly throughout a facility to avoid detection. As soon as all of this entered the prison, it should have been spread out among several members of the crew involved in its transport and distribution. The idea that a guy would be sitting on all of this contraband and rolling something at his desk just didn't seem right. He may have been preparing some tobacco or marijuana for distribution, but that didn't explain why the drugs and tobacco were all in the same prisoner's cell, just waiting to be discovered.

I knew that it was dangerous for us to have even discovered these items, and it was even more dangerous for the person who had been caught with them. Being the one who was caught with the contraband meant that you were the part of the chain that broke. From an outsider's perspective, that might mean you would be worried about your sentence being increased, but anyone who knows prison would tell you that the real thing you would be worried about was what your boss would have someone do to you for messing up. The other two correctional staff searching the room found a bag of pills containing about two hundred pills and a computer tablet. Yes, a computer tablet, right there in someone's room! The pills were given to the medical staff to find out what type of pills they were. We wanted to know right away if we were dealing with aspirin-level contraband or something more serious. It turned out that the pills were, indeed, not just someone's store of aspirin but various substances that could be used recreationally.

The next couple of days were among the most anxious and uncomfortable times I can remember, for both the staff and the prisoners. This was a major drug and cell phone bust of a major criminal enterprise that had been operating within this state correctional facility. The prisoner who was caught with all this contraband was just the tip of the iceberg, and everyone knew it. Both staff and prisoners knew that both staff and prisoners had to have been involved in the smuggling of so many restricted items, so no one was beyond suspicion, aside from the three of us who had made the discovery and the new inspector who had ordered the search.

I myself had worked twenty-seven years in the Department of Corrections, yet I had never come across anything like this, where so much was discovered all at once. I'm also quite sure that the other two corrections officers who were searching with me hadn't even considered that something like this was possible. The loss of all this contraband meant that someone, or possibly many people in the chain of smuggling contraband, had taken a gigantic financial loss, as well as a hit to their reputation and their enterprise's whole existence. This meant that somebody, or several people, were going to have to pay off that debt or make things right somehow.

It's important to note that at some point in everyone's life, they are going to come to a point where they need to make a decision about whether or not to be accountable to themselves and stand up for what's right or pass the buck. Turning in all of this contraband and pursuing it meant giving up a lot of comfort in the workplace, and it also meant dedicating a lot of hours to something that you knew might get you fired or make you unpopular or even get you hurt.

To many people it would be easier to turn away from this kind of discovery—the discovery of corruption in your workplace, whether it's a prison or a police department or a school or a business. To reveal corruption in any workplace means putting yourself at risk, and for a lot of people it's easier to turn a blind eye, to pretend that what they've discovered isn't that big of a deal, and to do nothing—that's how all of this works. People don't confront what's going on in their communities; they pretend not to notice even those problems wreaking havoc on their families. They do all this so that they don't make waves and usually for the sake of keeping their jobs, which just give them some crumbs. When you're willing to sacrifice what's right and good for your community, the community you live in becomes a more peaceful place for all to live in, and when you continue to turn a blind eye toward these things, that's when you know you've become a pawn for the system, which sometimes means that you start looking at others for a way out.

When we don't hold each other accountable or when we chose not to take a stand, even if it's in our own families, that's permitting more negative criminality to come our way. Taking a stance against negative actions that cause so much harm to your family and your community can bring about a more positive outcome for you and most likely the person bringing that negative vibe to you and your loved ones. After being placed in a position to go into that particular room to make this huge discovery, I knew I would have to follow up on any actions that came afterward. I was not about to forget what had happened or get lost in the day-to-day activities of the prison and hope that someone higher up would take care of it. I knew that if I was going to have any kind of peace of mind about this discovery I had been involved in, I'd have to see for myself that something was done about it. That's called integrity, accountability, and responsibility. I didn't ask for it but when put in this position, I have to follow through.

After this discovery, I did receive a lot of aggressive stares from prisoners, and I know that the other officers who had made similar major discoveries also received these threatening looks. But for the most part, prisoners understood and respected that if a correctional officer had a good reputation—of being fair and professional—and he wasn't involved in corruption, then he risked his entire career's reputation if he suddenly turned a blind eye to contraband. They understood that I had to turn in any contraband that I found. They also understood and respected that I was well respected within the prison facility and that I would not risk my entire career on this. This went a long way in terms of prisoners accepting that there had to be consequences to this discovery, and whatever amount they'd invested in the contraband that was discovered had to be chalked up as a loss.

Let me make this perfectly clear too: not all prisoners engage in drugs or in the selling or distribution of contraband. And those who do engage in it are being bullied or threatened into it, even though it's incredibly risky. A lot of guys from the different ethnicities want to get back home to their loved ones, and even those who deal in the illegal activities understand that if they're caught, it's on them. The main concern among the prisoners was whether or not another prisoner had told on them or not, and if it had been another prisoner, who was he? I knew that the most dangerous element in the contraband chain was not the discovery but who had told on them and punishing that person, so I still wasn't particularly worried about my safety. I knew that the prisoners all had an idea of who had unraveled their plans. The correctional facility is a small world, full of vigorous men who have very little to do. News travels fast. I wasn't under any illusions that the identities of the officers who had participated in this historical contraband bust would be a secret for long. Still, I knew that this wasn't the time anyone would act out violently against a corrections officer; they'd be more concerned with finding the snitch. If I was ever going to be worried about my safety, I would've been worried when I was working in a maximum-security facility with all those lifers around me.

The intrigue around the contraband discovery started right away. As soon as the contraband was discovered, it was placed on a table across from the control center. The control center was a correctional staff area. While several high-ranking supervisors (captains, lieutenants, and sergeants) in the area were viewing the contraband, the warden-king came into the room, glanced at the contraband, then looked at the new inspector for a moment. He looked around at the other staff but refused to look at me.

"Tape up these windows," the warden-king said to the other staff members, "I wouldn't want anyone to see this."

This was strange, because as I said news travels fast in a prison, and the area was secure from prisoners.

Then the warden-king turned to the inspector and said, "Come with me."

The inspector said nothing, but left the room with the warden-king. I was surprised but didn't think that much of it. There were plenty of reasons for these two to have a private conversation.

The other staff and I just left it at that. The supervisors, who were this warden-king regime's lieutenants (knights) and sergeants (rooks), did as they were told and put paper over all the windows so that this evidence couldn't be viewed by anyone. One of the warden's lieutenants (knights) pulled me to the side and said, "You should've come to me when you found that contraband." This made me wonder why?

This would lead me back to the bag of about ten to eleven empty, hollowed-out soap bars that were found on the top of the locker; it appeared the contraband from those bars of soap was already distributed throughout the correctional facility. All the items that were found were photographed, tickets were written up, and critical incident reports were written. The captain and the new inspector of the facility placed everything into the state police evidence box, which each correctional facility has. The inspector and the captain discussed the matter with the state police sergeant who came to the correctional facility the next day.

Some strange occurrences would happen in the next month and a half. On November 1, 2012, the inspector who was supervising the investigation of this major cell phone and drug bust was demoted to the rank of lieutenant. This was allegedly due to the downsizing or restructuring of the staff at the correctional facility, but it was extremely suspicious considering this particular inspector's role in the ongoing investigation that implicated the administration who had decided to demote him. The administration also said that the captain's position was no longer needed—once again, removing one of the key players in the contraband investigation. The administration claimed that these positions were no longer necessary, but maybe they meant that they didn't want anyone in these positions to pursue the investigation.

Was this an attempt to remove the two most powerful supervisors—inspector and captain—who were involved in prosecuting these contraband discoveries, or was this coincidental restructuring? I'm not sure. Additionally, at this time, at least eight hundred of the one thousand and fifty prisoners we had at our facility were immediately relocated to a prison in the lower, western part of Michigan. This was a majority of the prisoners, and strangely enough, there was not only a facility open, it also didn't take long to relocate these prisoners to that other facility. Suddenly Ryan Correctional Facility was under utterly new supervision and less than 80 percent of our original population of prisoners.

The administration at the other correctional facility was given a heads-up about what had been found at the prison previously, so they knew that they might be introducing some experienced smugglers into their population. I believe they held on to these prisoners' property for about a week to make sure that there was no contraband coming their way unexpectedly. Why such drastic changes so fast? I don't know. Was all this coincidental, or was our prison being completely rebooted? You make the call; one thing is for sure: things were unraveling fast.

Knowing that during the summer months and into the fall the metropolitan cities and communities were suffering the typical summer criminal activities (drugs, shootings, murders), when looking back on things, you could take some pride in knowing that hopefully your actions would stop the spread of violence that was going on. There's no way that prisoners in a correctional facility should have had this amount of contraband, cell phones especially, with which they could continue to run their criminal enterprises even from within the prison. Who knows what those cell phones were being used for—to manipulate judges, policemen, prosecutors, jurors, or witnesses? A discovery of this magnitude indicated that there was a certain comfort level within the prison. Most prisoners were smart and self-interested. They wouldn't undertake the risks in hiding and distributing this contraband if they weren't reasonably sure of their security. The fact that they were willing to take these risks inside the prison indicated that there was a comfort level with smuggling in Ryan Correctional Facility at that time. Amazingly to me, there was even some regime staff who saw me as a snitch or a rat. Of course there were also prisoners who viewed me that way, but that was understandable. I had disrupted their interests, and many of them had suffered a loss. Even the guy who just wanted to smoke a few cigarettes wasn't able to get them because of my bust. But the staff were supposed to be against contraband, and I definitely got the feeling from some staff that they viewed me as the bad guy. This environment had all been made possible by corrections staff not doing their jobs, overlooking certain matters, and this correctional facility was running wild under the reign of the regime.

By January 2013, which was now about three months after the discovery of the contraband, and shortly after the removal of the new inspector and captain who were both supervising the investigation of contraband, I became curious as to where they had sent both the state informant prisoner and the prisoner who had been caught with all of the contraband. To find this information, I just had to look up these prisoners on the Michigan Offender Tracking Information System (OTIS) website, which is the offender's search website. This website was a database of information pertaining to Michigan State prisoners. When I looked up these two prisoners, I found out some stunning details.

These two key prisoners were not only at the very same prison they were living in the same housing unit. They were both placed there on separate occasions by someone from the regime's correctional administration. How would I know this? Because after finding out that they were there, I contacted a former coworker, who was now at the same correctional facility as these two prisoners. I wanted to give him and his coworkers a heads-up that these two prisoners were not only involved in an ongoing contraband investigation, but that they were essentially on opposites sides of the situation, meaning that they had every reason to want to hurt each other. One had essentially gotten the other one caught, with a large amount of contraband, and now they were living in the same housing unit? Very strange indeed.

After looking on OTIS and finding that both these prisoners were in the same location, I requested information through the Freedom of

Information Act (FOIA). Specifically, I requested information about the tickets I had written about the contraband I had found. I wanted to see the official report with my own eyes.

I was shocked by what the FOIA returned to me. They only sent back information about one ticket, which dealt with the scalpel that I had found. There was no indication that anything else had been found during the search of this prisoner's room. According to the official report, there was no tobacco, no drugs, and no cell phones. Additionally, the report of the scapula downplayed its importance. The scalpel was very sharp, and I believe it was used to carve out hollow areas in the soap to hide the contraband. However, it was also a dangerous object for any prisoner to have when living in conditions of high stress and close proximity to other violent individuals. Yet the report I received through the FOIA classified the scalpel as a tool, not a weapon. This means that in the official report, this extremely sharp and dangerous tool was classified in the same category as a hammer or a wrench.

When I called and asked the person involved with the FOIA about the other tickets I had requested information about, the representative said to me, "We don't have anything else that you may have written."

I was shocked by this, because the most important tickets I had written were nowhere to be found. Someone had made them disappear. I was looking at the official record of my big cell phone and drug bust, but the only paperwork I could find on it was about the discovery of the scalpel, and even that was classified incorrectly, as a tool instead of a weapon. Now it appeared as if nothing had happened at our correctional facility. Was all this a coincidence too? I knew that it was impossible for those important tickets to have been inadvertently misplaced, especially when they were potential evidence against a criminal enterprise; something smelled rotten about this.

The majority of Ryan's prisoners had been transferred out, including the two prisoners involved in the investigation; they were transferred to Macomb prison. A lot of the staff at the Macomb Facility had worked with me at Mound Correctional Facility before that facility closed. At that time, half our team had transferred to Macomb, while the other half went to Ryan. It was surprising that the one prisoner caught with the contraband wouldn't be sent to a higher custody level? What was the purpose of sending both prisoners to the same correctional facility and into the same housing unit? You might guess what happened next. One of the prisoners "shanked" or stabbed the other. No one was seriously hurt, and the two were then transferred yet again, away from that facility.

Now, let me make this perfectly clear: prisoners are going to do what they do. They'll fight, manipulate, and find someone else to do it for them if they can't. It has to be understood that that's going to happen. But when you have an administrative staff incompetently putting people in harm's way, that's what is unacceptable. They not only put these two individuals in a dangerous situation but also put every staff member at that facility in harm's way. If the staff had not been prepared and warned about these two prisoners, the violent exchange between them could have gone even further, and they could have gotten hurt more seriously. Additionally, any time there is a potential problem between prisoners, it is a possible source of harm and danger for correctional staff too. When prisoners are willing to hurt each other, they go into the fight prepared to get in trouble, with their emotions taking over. This means they are more willing to hurt guards if they get in the way of the prisoners getting out their emotions through violence.

Of course, the most disturbing part of this situation is the possibility that these two prisoners were placed in the same housing unit with the hope that they might hurt each other. If either of these prisoners was hurt, they wouldn't be able to say what they knew about the contraband ring. The administration would know that the prisoner who was caught with the contraband would be especially willing to hurt the snitch, which would benefit the staff involved with the contraband ring. Not to mention that, with the disappearance of the tickets, it seems that more was done to hide the situation than was done to address what went wrong and prevent it from happening again.

If prevention was on anyone's mind, these two individuals would have been sent to the next step up the security level. Someone, or several people, from the regime knew that putting these two prisoners in the same housing unit was wrong and that it was likely that one would try to hurt the other and possibly the two would even end up killing each other. At the very least, they should be in higher custody levels because they were involved in an investigation that implicated the correctional department staff.

When classifying prisoners for custody levels, most corrections officers know it takes four administrative staffers to have that meeting. Was it the warden-king and his knights or his rooks or his pawns on that panel? Maybe the whole panel was made up of people in whose interest it was for these two prisoners to fight and harm each other and further indicate that they were problematic prisoners whose testimonies were not to be trusted.

Three weeks later, after finding all of this out, I knew that the corruption in this situation was a lot more than I could handle on my own. It was time to protect myself. I filed a Hostile Work Environment/Interfering with a Criminal Investigation Complaint against the warden-king and the new deputy warden (bishop). I didn't know exactly who all the players were or exactly how dangerous this situation could become. I needed to look ahead and be aware that I was almost assuredly outnumbered by the regime's officers, and they had the advantage of me not knowing who they were, even while I was exposed, since everyone knew I was asking questions.

I was not about to be a pawn or a sacrificial lamb in this game of checkers. Why do I say checkers? Because this surely was not a game of chess; in checkers, you have chips that you just bounce around without much thought and without much risk. All the pieces are the same, so there's no real strategy. You just move the pieces around. In chess, you move strategically; you pay attention to each move in order to get the best move this round but also the better move down the road. They might have thought they were playing chess, but it would come out that they were playing checkers with people's lives. To these men, the prisoners were just pieces to be moved around on a whim or to be used for personal gain, with no thought of the prisoners as human beings.

I have to believe that the administration at the other facility was furious that they were blindsided by this regime, after finding out that such a dangerous situation had been placed in their hands with no warning.

In response to my official complaint about a hostile work environment, I received a disappointing letter from the Internal Affairs Division of the state. The letter stated, "This does not appear to be discriminatory harassment, i.e., weight, height, race, although there may appear to be work rule violation. You have to take this matter up with your administrative staff." Basically, they advised me to make the complaint to the people who I was complaining against. I knew that this actually meant, "We're done with this matter." This was a swift two weeks after filing a complaint.

No one in Internal Affairs would touch these serious allegations for months, not until September 2013. No phone calls, no face-to-face interviews, nothing happened. On three different occasions between March 2013 and July 2013, I spoke to the sergeant who supervised the correctional facility and was in charge of the investigation. I asked him what was going on with the investigation, but each time I talked to him, he dismissed me. He seemed to be dry, full of loathing about talking about these issues. He would talk to me briefly and say that it was under investigation and that he knew who the new inspector was who gave him the investigation packet. On the third try, I called another state police office post to try to find out from a lieutenant at that state police post what was going on with the investigation. When I made that call, I was transferred back to that sergeant by a reception staff.

That's when I decided to go straight to the top, to the Lansing State Police Headquarters with my complaint. It was clear that just asking questions to anyone in the Department of Corrections was discouraged, and that no one there was going to give me the information I was looking for. By contacting the state police in Lansing, I thought, surely I would get the ball rolling. If not, I thought, at least somebody would have my side of the story.

By August 2013, I had sent letters out to the attorney general's desk, the Department of Corrections, which had already received all the information much earlier, the Wayne County Prosecutor's Public Corruption Advisory, and three different local news media outlets, as well as the FBI investigative team. At this point, it was just about whether or not these people from the regime were playing checkers or chess. We were about to find out if the regime were truly gangsters in their ways and actions. All these pieces were placed together on the board, but it was unclear what the next move would be. I was surely not playing checkers, bouncing around from one place to another, not understanding what was going on. I knew the consequences of my actions, and I was prepared to accept them. I had done everything in my power to notify the powers that be of what was happening, and when those powers didn't respond, I went higher up. I didn't think there was much higher to go, so now all that was left for me to do was wait to see what this variety of powerful people would do with all this information.

I knew that if and when these professional law enforcement units inquired about the investigation, someone was going to have to be held accountable for what they had done, while others might find themselves accountable for what they had not done.

Around September 25, 2013, I was called to the control-center area to retrieve a call with the area code 517, from the new deputy warden (bishop)'s office. It turned out that I was finally going to speak with the Internal Affairs Division of the Department of Corrections. Now, they wanted to talk to me about the whole investigative complaint.

The first thing they asked me on the call was, "Are you in the office by yourself?"

"Yes," I said.

Then they asked if I minded being put on speaker phone.

"Sure," I said, because I had nothing to hide. I was glad to finally get my story heard. I wanted whoever was in the room at Internal Affairs Office to hear what I had to say. I spoke about the incident, from beginning to end, and they listened. When I got to the discovery of all the contraband, the drugs, and cell phones, the internal affairs supervisor interrupted me.

"I thought I had seen all the tickets," he said in disbelief.

"No," I told him. "I requested all of those tickets through the FOIA, and only one ticket came back to me. Of the many tickets I wrote on the day of the incident, only one showed up in the official records."

I explained what I had found out from the FOIA and how the scalpel had been classified as a tool and how the most important tickets had just disappeared.

Then the internal affairs supervisor struggled and stumbled over his words.

"Well," he said, "I don't know much about custody levels and how all this paperwork gets moved around..."

So he was trying to pass the buck too. This annoyed me, and I said, "Why are you even in that position if you don't know anything about custody levels?" Now I was on a roll and finally able to confront the incompetence I had been witnessing throughout this whole process. If the internal affairs supervisor thought it was a joke about him not knowing much about custody levels, he would soon get very quiet.

"Look," I said, "The whole reason for having custody levels is that some prisoners are more capable of constantly getting in trouble, catching major ticket violations while in prison, while others were simply not into getting in trouble; they were trying to get out of prison and back to their loved ones. How could you not place someone involved in such a high-impact contraband situation in a higher level of custody after you found out that they were capable of this level of smuggling? Most law enforcement staff, as well as any competent citizen, could make that judgment call."

Remember, I was on speaker phone and there was someone from the state police office present, someone from the Department of Corrections, and who knows who else was in that room at the time. I heard some of them stifling mumbling when I spoke about the supervisor not knowing much about custody levels. I heard a few of them burst out laughing, but the laughter subsided quickly when I went on to talk about my twenty-seven years of service in the Department of Corrections and how this level of incompetence was unheard of.

The internal affairs supervisor stumbled again over his words and tried to tell me to have a nice day—that they had my number—and then he hung up the phone.

That was the only time I talked to anyone in the Department of Corrections administration for the first year after the incident took place it was a year later. It probably would have been interesting to know who was in the room with the internal affairs supervisor when I told him what was what. I didn't care about being polite anymore, and I had nothing to hide. I just wanted to hold these men accountable for the dangerous position they were putting myself and my coworkers in every day, perhaps by sheer incompetence. They were playing a game of checkers when they should have been playing chess.

There is something to be learned from those who straddle the fence between right and wrong. These administrators wanted to believe that all of this corruption happening on their watch had nothing to do with them, but if they had been doing their jobs, who knows how many cell phone calls from prisoners could have been stopped.

Those phones were almost certainly used for criminal activity, which could have included murder and the covering up of murder. These administrators don't believe their actions have anything to do with those murders, but their incompetence allowed all that contraband to flow through the prison for who knows how long. Even those correctional staff who were materially benefiting from the smuggling were not helping themselves, they were just pawns in someone's game. If you're not helping the cause against violence and crime, you're just hurting your own community. They believed they were in control, but they were just peeking around the corner, not knowing what was really going on.

On November 4, 2013, in the midevening hours, three individuals, I assume from the Director of Corrections' office, came to the correctional facility and escorted the warden-king off the grounds. They also confiscated his hard drive and put the new deputy warden in as the interim warden. This became effective immediately, that very day. Why so abruptly?

I didn't know why; all I knew was that when I got to work the next morning, it was eerily quiet. The regime had been completely toppled now, and one of my fellow coworkers who had worked at the other facility with me hollered out, "Why is everybody so quiet this morning?"

I smiled. We both knew that it was because the warden-king was gone. Now the rest of his chess pieces would start to fall, and the regime would collapse. This game of checkers that was being played had come to an end. Panic would soon set in among the others lieutenants (knights), sergeants (rooks), and corrections officers (pawns), and by the next month, it was all revealed.

By December 2, 2013, three weeks after the warden-king was escorted out of the correctional facility, one of his lieutenants (knights) came up to me while I was on my assignment. He confessed to me that he and a sergeant (rook) had been told to dispose of the items we'd found in the cell phone, pills, and drug bust. They were given this order by the new deputy warden (bishop) per a conversation with the warden (king). The lieutenant (knight) went on to say, "There was some sensitive stuff in the evidence box," but that he was told, "Just do it."

I asked the lieutenant (knight), "Why are you just now telling me this, after being my immediate supervisor for the last fourteen months, and knowing full well what the ramifications were?" I told him, "You know I'm going to document this."

This same lieutenant (knight) had previously told me that he was "glad not to be involved in any of it during the time of the contraband being found," but now, when faced with the possibility of me reporting him, he said, "I don't care if they don't like me anyway."

I documented the conversation and sent it to Internal Affairs; of course, I would not hear back from them, but that was okay.

Hmmm…checkmate!
Did I feel some vindication at this time? Yes.
Was I jumping with joy? No.

That's not who I am. I truly believe that I was being used by the man upstairs in Heaven to teach some people some valuable lessons about power, false power, accountability, and truthfulness. I was just a vessel being used to show other correctional staff members the power of coming together, because this just wasn't about me. Other people played a great part in helping to topple the regime that was harassing everyone, creating a hostile work environment for all staff.

The Department of Corrections did its best to smother the story and avoid the public relations nightmare that this would have brought about if the citizens of this metropolitan area knew what was going on inside this correctional facility at the time. Remember, the tax payers of Michigan were paying the tab for all of this corruption and all of this wasted time that could have been spent rooting out the criminal activities and making these state institutions safer for everyone inside them. Tax payers were paying for prisoners to be rehabilitated, not for prisoners to be used as pawns by staff to further their personal power trips.

The correctional facility had changed over to a parole violation center one year before toppling the regime. So we were now transitioning to dealing with the lowest custody level prisoners. These prisoners were within six months or less of being paroled and placed back in their communities.

There were no letters sent to me by any members of the director's office or himself. I was okay with that. My accountability came from working with some truly professional staff in my early years and knowing how a correctional institution hierarchy should function. Even though the ones supervising me thought they were safe in their power abuses, their safety depended on no one questioning them or their actions. They expected all the staff to be pawns, to be unquestioning sheep that would just do what we were told. But I was not going to be that pawn that they expected me to be—the pawn who offers up his life like a sacrificial lamb to protect the needs of the king.

Here is the time line of events that would eventually be the demise of the king and his pieces,

Timeline of Events from September 2012 to December 2012. September 24, 2012: Two other Corrections Officers and myself were called to the inspector's office to read a letter from a prisoner that his ex-bunkmate had drugs, cell phones, a homemade cuff key, and weapons and that the ex-bunkmate wanted to kill a corrections officer. We were ordered to search the prisoner's room and find the "mother lode of all contraband." We did a write-up and reported the contraband through appropriate official channels.

September 25, 2012: During a second sweep of the room, I discovered that four of the bars of soap contained Motorola flip phones, two bars of soap had clean plastic bags in each, with marijuana clearly visible, two more bars of soap had two clear plastic bags in each with gray duct tape wrapped around each substance, allegedly cocaine, the last two bars of soap contained two purple gloves, each containing an unknown substance, which was allegedly heroine. All this contraband was laid out on a table, and the inspector, warden, lieutenants, sergeants, C/S, and parole supervisor all verified its existence. Total number of phones found was six, and the total number of alleged drug bars of soap was six.

September 28, 2012: All these items were photographed, tickets were written, critical incident reports were written and given to the state police sergeant, who saw the items. Items and reports were placed in the state police evidence box at Ryan Correctional Facility. Both inspector and then captain were in contact with the state police.

November 1, 2012: The inspector was demoted to a lieutenant due to an alleged downsizing and restructuring of staff at the Ryan/Detroit Detention Center. This is where I believe that the administration at Ryan/Detroit Reentry Detention Center started to and conspired to do away with the evidence of a major drugs and cell phone operation going on at the facility. They were able to get the inspector and the captain out of the way due to the restructuring of supervisory staff by the warden.

January 20, 2013: I found out where the prisoners were through OTIS. I also found out that only one ticket was included in the official report and that all the reports of the drugs and phones had disappeared.

February 5, 2013: I filed a Hostile Work Environment/Interfering with a Criminal Investigation Whistle-blower lawsuit complaint against the warden and the deputy warden of the Ryan/Detroit Reentry Detention Center in Detroit, Michigan. This was sent out through the proper channels, through EEOR and given to the Internal Affairs Division.

February 20, 2013: Internal Affairs replied to my complaint but will not follow up on it.

March 3, 2013–July 30, 2013: I speak to administrative staff on three different occasions about the state of the investigation and am dismissed every time.

September 3, 2013: I sent out three certified letters to the Attorney General's Office of the State of Michigan, the state police in Lansing, Michigan, and the Wayne County Prosecutor's Public Corruptions Division about why there wasn't any active investigation into the contraband discovery.

September 25, 2013: I was called by Internal Affairs, and I told them everything I knew about the discovery and the cover-up.

November 14, 2013: Three individuals arrived at Ryan and escorted the warden off the premises.

December 2, 2013: A supervisor admits to me that he had "disposed" of all the contraband, which he was ordered to do by the warden-king and the bishop.

December 5, 2013: I sent another Hostile Work Environment Complaint to the EEOC and to the Internal Affairs Department based on the information the supervisor had given me on Dec. 2.

As of December 8, 2013: No one had been fired or reprimanded for their actions; everyone was able to retire and collect a pension from the State of

Michigan. They would make a token gesture of having a disciplinary investigation as of January 2014, but the problem with that was the regime boss had retired a month earlier. I would go on to retire one year later on March 31, 2015. I had no problems come my way during any of this time period probably because I had a high-profile lawyer from Detroit who was well known; he had just got his client a substantial amount of money from the City of Detroit in a lawsuit, due to the then mayor's actions. This is probably why I never got a call from the Department of Corrections at all.

## Chapter 6

# CONCLUSION: I WILL NOT BE A PAWN

Why is all this corruption covered up? The sad truth is that if prisons are run as corporations, for profit rather than rehabilitation, then it's to the prison's benefit if the prisoners are *not* rehabilitated. It means that prisoners' stays are extended, or they are released and turn back to crime, and they return as prisoners again. More prisoners mean more contracts, more kickbacks for the administrators, and ultimately, job security for anyone in the corrections field.

At one point the administration gave a contract to a clearly inferior food service company, and this did real damage and caused some real health problems. The department decided that they wanted to feed the prisoners at a cheaper cost. As a result, 325 food service supervisors throughout the state were "laid off." Their jobs were "absorbed," and they had no recourse. They were given the option to be corrections officers, but they had to pass a physical. Most of these food service men and women had twenty years or more on the job, and they couldn't pass the required physical, which was geared toward young people coming into the system. Only about twenty food supervisors passed the test, so the bottom line resulted in three hundred lost jobs.

When these food service supervisors were removed, of course the quality of the food for prisoners dipped substantially. The food wasn't prepared properly, they paid people half as much, and they received zero benefits for working in the correctional facility. They brought men and women off the streets into a really manipulative, complicated setting, without adequate training. These new people didn't seem to know what they were doing. There were maggots in the food. Now, of course the prison isn't supposed to be a four-star hotel, but no judge ever sentenced anyone to having maggots in their food. If children have maggots in their food, it's because someone is neglecting them. These prisoners were being neglected. Additionally, the women were starting to date the prisoners. The new female food employees were coming into a correctional facility looking for prisoners to date. It was truly a sad; these women would go get their hair and nails done to impress these prisoners, not knowing the dangerous situations they were placed in trying to find a mate. This kind of practice was happening throughout the state, not just at one correctional facility. Three years later they did away with that food service contract.

You may be wondering how could all that happen during the time period where there were workshops and educational material, classroom training on employee and prisoner relations, and hostility training being conducted throughout the state and country on these matters. Sometimes when you give egotistical individuals unchecked power, you're going to run into these sort of problems. Again, at the initial start of all this foolishness, I wasn't targeted. I happened to be a keen observer and have a ton of experience and understanding of how a correctional facility should be properly run by administrative staff. This was unacceptable. Remember, a large majority of the staff came from Mound Correctional Facility and bumped out Ryan's lower-seniority staff, so we had some leverage. A lot of the staff from Ryan who were left behind didn't feel comfortable with that, even though we were all corrections officers inside of the same prison who should be working together for one common goal: protecting the public from the dangers that lurk within these settings.

You may or may not be aware of a lot of the problems going on in your community and throughout the country that come about from within the prison or correctional settings. A lot of decisions and actions on the outside derive directly from calls being made from the inside. That is why it was so disturbing to know that when such a large amount of contraband was revealed by one of the informants, nothing was done about it. It was tough to go about as though none of this had ever happened. They discarded the evidence and put correctional staff in very dangerous situations; none of this should be tolerated at any level of criminal justice or corrections system.

I don't know what these individuals were thinking about, but I was thinking about the safety of citizens in the metropolitan communities that were around this prison. I often thought about how many lives were being damaged due to the large number of cell phones that were smuggled into this facility. They were in the hands of individuals doing life in prison and those doing long stints of ten to twenty-five years or fifteen to forty years, who could be using these phones to knock off witnesses, judges, police, or other citizens of the metropolitan areas.

The ultimate turning point for me was the situation of the letter or kite about killing a corrections officer and the administrative staff not taking this matter seriously. Knowing that this could have been any one of us, corrections officers, who were only doing our part in these institutions, here's a question I would like answered: Why would anyone send their state informant to the same prison, the same housing unit, as the guy who got in trouble because of this informant? Unless you're completely incompetent, I don't know why you would make that decision. Was there something else to this we don't know about?

Was it all done by design? We will never know. Those administrative people and supervisors were able to walk away and just retire—even at the top. You may ask, aren't you scared to write this book? But I'm not I'm just the messenger sent by the man up above.

At one point during all this mess, one of my coworkers came up to me and said, "You know what, man? This isn't coming from you; this is coming from the man upstairs. You were put in that situation by him to stop all of this nonsense that was taking place."

I stopped and thought for a minute. It was probably true, what he had said, because I had always been respected by my peers and by prisoners themselves not only for my fairness but also for my constant positive-reinforcement attitude. I didn't ask for this particular assignment, but once I was put in this position as part of my job, I would do it.

Let me say that not all convicts have bad intentions. For the last two and a half years, I've watched some very positive things happening inside the prison walls. In addition to all these unethical, murky situations of corruption, there have also been stories of redemption and deliverance.

The group who worked with youth offenders had youth coming from as far as Toledo, Ohio; Kalamazoo, Michigan; Flint, Pontiac, and other areas around Metropolitan Detroit. Their guidance, information, and honest approach about life influenced countless young people across the region. There were seven or eight prisoners who did amazing work through this program, even to this day. One well-known news writer named Garrett helped to put the program together, and it is still running to this day.

These are the type of programs that should have been highlighted and talked about more often. Here you have a group of prisoners who are willing to tell these young men about their wrongdoings to help improve their lives. I'm sure it is therapeutic for the prisoners who run it also. And on that point, this leads me to the older adult prisoners who should be given every opportunity to slow this mass incarceration of youthful offenders into prisons. There are mature, wise prisoners who can have positive effects on youth, and these individuals, if properly screened, should be favorably considered for parole. I'm not saying that those who have committed despicable, unjustifiable acts should be set free, but those who are much older than they were when they came in, senior citizens who are truly remorseful and show these signs, could truly make a difference in outside communities, given the opportunity.

One former prisoner eventually ran for city council. He went in for murder, did ten years, and got out, and his family was very supportive of him. Eventually he became a motivational speaker, and he was on TV shows, motivating other teenagers to go down the right path in life. These kids would be as young as ten, boys and girls, and he'd be on that show to talk to the kids and straighten them up. He just missed out on a seat on the city council in Detroit.

One inmate who showed a very serious positive attitude toward correcting his behavior was a young man who wore a Sherlock Holmes hat, a two-sided cap. He also went on to make something of himself. He had stuck out to me in the halfway house correctional setting (where prisoners were able to be released back into their communities after ninety days) because of his hat and because of an incident when a female guard and I let the prisoners have a rap or poetry contest because they were behaving so well. During the evening hours, after they had completed their evening meal, before they went back to their rooms, at least four residents from each floor competed with each other one by one, standing inside a circle, spitting (singing) out lyrics, which was their poetry; they didn't need any music at all. The residents wanted to do this, and my coworker and I were okay with it because it wasn't harming anyone and had a positive effect on the residents. Rapping or voicing poetry in front of an audience, with a sense of competition, gave the residents a sense that their words and creativity were being appreciated and respected. They were able to express themselves, get their feelings out, and feel a sense of accomplishment at delivering their art before an audience.

After eight residents had finished their raps and poetry from each floor, I was sure that my residents had won the contest, but in the background, out of the blue came the resident with the Sherlock Holmes two-sided cap. He got in the middle of the circle and performed some lyrics, really smoothly and precisely. It lasted about five minutes, and afterward you could see the other residents with their mouths dropped open and eyes frozen with attention. My coworker and I looked at each other and said, "Where did that come from?"

The resident in the Sherlock Holmes hat just shrugged it off and told us that he was a rapper. I said, "A rapper? You are about nineteen years old, coming from a corrections setting; how is that possible?"

Well, I was surprised to learn that this guy really was in the rap industry. As the years went on and even after four months of being released and placed on parole, this young man with the Sherlock Holmes hat was making a video and had recorded a rap album. To this day, I hear his voice on the radio locally, representing insurance companies and doing other radio advertising. He's a prominent figure in the rap industry here in Detroit Michigan and known as Detroit's own gangster rapper. He hangs out with Eminem and other famous artists. When he was a resident, he would talk to other parolee prisoners who were locked up and use positive reinforcement and encouragement in his communications with other residents during his brief stay.

Fifteen years later, I ran into this Detroit rapper on one occasion at a local fitness gym, where he was talking to one of the trainers he knew, and sure enough, he remembered that experience of the rap-off and thanked me for not being judgmental and letting the guys have a release valve at that time. This reminded me of the important influence that can come from meeting the right people in troubling situations.

Sometimes young men need a vision, a way to look forward toward something positive; there are opportunities that are out there for them to strive for. Too many times, young men settle for underperforming jobs instead of career-oriented jobs. But they must first remain focused in order to put themselves in a position to achieve a career. What do I mean by that? There must not be a lot of distraction and turmoil going on. If at all possible, girlfriends, homeboys, and family distractions need to be pushed to the side. One must always try to maintain a positive outlook and have the mind-set to pursue achievements.

You may be wondering why you see these young men walking around with their pants hanging off their behinds or butts. This does not come from your state correctional facilities; you'd better not try that in the prison setting. It may come from your local lockups, due to the fact that the first forty-eight to seventy-two hours of lockup are stressful times, as they will take your belts and shoestrings. When you see those young men in their sagging pants, it's a cry of "Where's my father?" Because Lord knows no father that I know, or any father, would step up to the plate and stop this nonsense. After working in the correction system for over twenty-nine years and talking to thousands of prisoners and counselors, I have concluded that a man or woman will only change if he or she wants to. The criminal justice system is a very complex system; from the time an individual makes a conscious choice to commit a crime, is caught, and goes to trial, he or she pays a costly price. The police, the court system, the corrections system, and the vendors all cost the tax payers billions of dollars. The real question is?, how can we reduce or eliminate this revolving-door game? What is a viable solution? It's going to take a combination of groups interfacing to deal with these complex issues; law enforcement, prosecutors, judges, social workers, and family members must all come together to assist in ridding society of these social ills. Churches also must play a major role in telling their congregations the truth about their sons, daughters, uncles, and aunts. Family members and girlfriends must stop enabling these law breakers who continue on their paths without any consequences; antisocial behavior can no longer be expected or tolerated. Individuals must learn early that they cannot victimize members of society without being held responsible for their actions by their loved ones. When loved ones notify the authorities of the criminality of an individual, they may really be helping that individual out.

There is a war out on the streets, and when you have a war going on, you need every available source of trustworthy manpower and knowledge to help you, if you're truly trying to stop the violence.

Let me reiterate: prisoners are going to find things to do to break up the boredom of their daily routines. That's understandable in this setting. You expect that prisoners will have contraband, illegally brought in, which they shouldn't have. You expect corrections officers and other noncustody correctional staff to be on the lookout for these kinds of things. We work for the taxpayers, and we are accountable to them, as we have authority over prisoners.

One thing you don't expect is that the administration will play games with people's lives. Again, I don't know everyone who was involved in this corruption or incompetence, but the director's office was surely in damage control mode after a while. We've seen this story time and time again, when absolute power corrupts absolutely.

False power unchecked leads to inhumane treatment, hostile work environments, and dangerous situations for everyone involved. You only need to look at some recent events, like the housing-market crash, where banks abused their power, or the water crisis in Flint, or the governing corruption in schools and city halls across the country. So it's not that it's surprising. I just didn't think I would be brought into this kind of mess in the very institution that was meant to rehabilitate criminals.

I believe I was chosen because I'm one of the most respected corrections officers who did his job and effectively communicated with prisoners in a positive manner. With my younger coworkers, I was always trying to help them see a more positive side of things while being in this negative environment. I would keep myself physically and mentally healthy—something one must do in order to have a healthy attitude when dealing with others.

No two officers are going to see the same thing due to their upbringing and experiences in life. But everyone must show professionalism when dealing with other ethnicities. Respect is essential in a corrections setting; the prisoner can see through staff being phony, favoring one or another. It may get the corrections officers some cool points for a while, but in the end they're setting themselves up for a big fall and even the possibility of getting manipulated and used without knowing it.

In this fast-paced capitalist society we live in, it's almost impossible not to know someone who is either locked up or who has been locked up, whether it was for a short period of time or a long period. People from all walks of life have been and will be locked up for a variety of reasons. Keeping prisons safe and effective is in the whole society's best interest. Prisoners being released back to their communities need to look square into that mirror and not be scared to change their ways.

When returning to the community, you need to do is own up to your responsibilities, which you've never done before. Even if you're locked up, look at the damage you've done to your family; you've left them out in the community to fend for themselves, while at the same time asking them to put money into your prison account. How about telling them that you're sorry for the troubles you've brought on them?

Most of the guys I came across were pretty much the breadwinners in their families, the go-getting hustlers with the ability to think outside the box but not applying those skills toward more positive, legit careers. There are some very thoughtful individuals who are locked up, and they need to start spreading the true wisdom they've acquired to these young men and woman who are left to grow up with many of their male role models locked up. These young men are playing checkers with their lives when the game of life involves chess. This mess that's going on now—random shootings, anger-management problems, and disrespectful behavior—is very alarming, and it's a reflection of the teaching within the family unit that has gone wrong.

Guys in prison, whether they like it or not, still have an obligation to the generations who follow them. They need to take a serious look in the mirror and ask themselves, "Do I continue to be part of the problem while I'm in here, or do I try to be part of the solution?" That's why I made it a point to emphasize the Youth Deterrent Program. These individuals—True-X, Spoon, Woody, Y-Blood, and several other prisoners—are truly giving back what they can to the young men who are out in the community confused and lost. They are trying to stop the flow of lost young men, and they don't have to do this; they want to do it.

I'd like to take this time to offer thoughts and prayers to the victims of violent crimes and their families, who have to endure the burden emotionally and financially after such acts occur to them and their families. No one should ever be comfortable with violent crimes and violent behavior in their communities. Those who sit back and see these violent behaviors unfold will never get their blessings.

During the mid-1980s, you could see the heavy influence of drugs working in the communities. There wasn't much one individual could do to stop it, but the one thing that the community and families needed to do was not to take the prison-mentality approach as a way of life; many people started accepting that it was okay to go in and out of prison, not understanding that carbon monoxide (silent killing gas) was creeping deeper into their communities. What I mean by the prison mentality is that every single thing, such as bumping into another person, staring at another person, or envying a person for no reason are very negative attitudes and become their mind-set. Manipulative behaviors out in the streets, total disrespect for authority figures, disrespect for the older members of the community—these are all part of a prison mentality.

The communities outside the prison started to accept these behavioral patterns as normal, and it just kept on creeping into the everyday lives of those who hadn't served time. Look at the saggy-pants syndrome, that crying out for a father, because surely no man would allow his son, or daughter, for that matter, to leave the house like that.

Some people say that this mentality comes from state penitentiaries, but I believe it comes as much from local lockups. These are places where they take your belts and your shoestrings when you get there, because of what is known as the "seventy-two-hour effect," when prisoners are at high risk of committing suicide during their first seventy-two hours in prison due to the shock of being confined, which is so stressful that prisoners are on automatic suicide watch.

I don't think you want to have saggy pants inside a correctional setting. Bigfoot Larry or Horse Boy would be waiting. Neither one would be a good option. We know that mental health is a major concern. Whoever came up with the concept of closing the mental-health facilities throughout the country did a hell of a job of disguising their true agenda and leaving communities with group homes, which would further overcrowd hospitals throughout the country with the mentally ill. Instead of getting the treatment they need, the mentally ill are often imprisoned, adding to the numbers and the contracts and the kickbacks. This is called corporate greed. That's playing chess, strategizing on how to make maximum profits from corporate investments by closing mental-health facilities.

That along with allowing these young men in inner cities who continue conducting themselves in these violent ways, playing checkers with their lives, bouncing around until the pieces fall right off the board, into the correctional system. The chess game is called "Corporate America," which profits from corporate prisons, making the people pawns in its system. One must be able to step out of the bubble and see things for what they're truly worth. Everyone is not going to be an athlete or a rap star or a reality TV star or even a hustler; there must be other options on the chess table: plumbers, electricians, and health-care professionals. There must be strategies that work—simple fundamentals of life, tried and true. For one thing, anyone who thinks they're going to make it without putting in the proper work is a foolish person. Trouble is the easiest thing to get into and the hardest thing to get out of. If individuals applied that same dress code they use when they are in the presence of a judge in his courtroom—white dress shirt and slacks (pants)—on a moderate to regular basis, just think of how different their view of life could be. If they could apply that same image and positive look back on the streets and in their neighborhoods and not just to impress the judge when being sentenced in the court, there would be far more opportunities for them.

Attitudes and your outlook toward life are very important. That's chess being played. What is your life's résumé? You are life's résumé cannot consist of traveling down the road of incarceration time and time again and then looking for a bailout later on. A life's résumé opens doors for you. If people see that you are attempting to stay positive, you will eventually receive some good blessings; therefore, one must always try and stay positive even when confronted with negativity, whether it's from family or friends.

I'd like to make one point perfectly clear: not all correctional facility deputy wardens, inspectors, or wardens are irresponsible or naïve. There are a tremendous number of correctional department administrators that I have worked with—some in the Upper Peninsula, the western part of Michigan, the thumb area, Middle Michigan area, and Macomb, Michigan, area—whom I hold in high regard for doing a great job. Seventy percent of the staff, both custodial and noncustodial food services staff, have always been very positive and congratulatory of my work, because they knew that the way people were behaving was wrong, and I didn't have any bad feedback from the folks who were there. They treated me like a hero. And a lot of them want to express their own feelings about what was going on through me writing this book. This book is about holding those in powerful, authoritative positions accountable for very dangerous positions they put correctional staff in. Shame on the Department of Corrections at the very top for not following through when they first got wind of this! It took fourteen months after being pressured to have them send some folks down in black Escalades to take a hard drive from the warden's office and escort him off the premises. One thing I tried to always do was stay professional at all times when dealing with prisoners, because you never know when you're going to see them again. Sometimes I would run into prisoners who have been released; they might see me out in the community or at my work site, and a lot of guys will call me over and want to introduce their families: girlfriend, wives, and children. One guy was in the hospital where I work, with his daughter and his girlfriend, because his daughter was sick, and he wanted to introduce them to me. Some guys who were locked up for life because of drug laws, who have had to serve nineteen years or more, have been released when the laws were changed, and these guys will walk up to me enthusiastically to say hello and tell me about their release. I know that they don't greet all the corrections officers this way when they see them in public, and it makes me feel like I must have done a good job if the prisoners who were in my care want to greet me and share their rehabilitation progress with me.

So in closing the story of my journey in corrections, I can say that I've met a lot of professional, determined coworkers who are and were doing a tremendous job. I've learned along the way that officers are somewhat like role models to those individuals who are under their care, who are truly trying to become better people. I learned that there are very knowledgeable prisoners who are locked up and come from all different backgrounds and ethnicities and that we all have some problems. Communications within any community between older and younger people is very vital. The young people have to know that you are sincere in your communication with them. They will see through fakeness. You must be careful when looking down at any individual, because you could possibly be put in a lockup situation yourself. How would you want to be treated? Here's my reflection on the end of my corrections journey.

In the game of chess, the pawns on the board can be the most powerful pieces at your disposal if used correctly. Used incorrectly, pawns can be the sacrificial lamb within the game. Those individuals at the Ryan Correctional Facility, who were playing checkers when the game of life is chess, began to unravel when the staff from the correctional facility from Mound arrived. That staff didn't ask for anything other than to do their job and were confronted with a lot of harassment and hostility. But in the end, the regime would begin tumbling down. None of the people involved in the corruption would be held accountable. They were all able to retire and move on with their lives. I'm quite sure they did learn a valuable lesson about common decency and false power when it comes to being in a powerful position.

Even at the very top of the administrative ladder, some folks were removed and allowed to go on to other careers, whereas the prisoners they had neglected never received such a second chance. I had no problems with those people who retired, as long as I knew that lessons were taught along the way about false power and deceit. It's a breath of fresh air to know that you can help your coworkers during troubling times. This story had to be told so that others in positions of power can know that it is wrong to use such unnecessary false power for their own selfish way. Subordinates in a corrections setting should also be mindful of and respectful of the power and responsibility that comes with their titles. There's always a higher power looking down on us; we all may come across times in our life where we must stand up for something, I would not be a sacrificial pawn, nor would I be used by the warden (king) or his queen or his bishop to be the little piece that their whole plan hinged on. I was my own man. I refused to be a pawn.

44184793R00060

Made in the USA
Middletown, DE
04 May 2019